MACRAMÉ FOR BEGINNERS

UNLOCKING MACRAMÉ MASTERY: ESSENTIAL TECHNIQUES FROM BASIC KNOTS TO BEAUTIFUL CREATIONS FOR MODERN CREATIVES"

Thelma Hammond

EXTRA BONUS!!!!

ECO MATERIALS GUIDE

READ TO THE END AND SCAN THE QR CODE

Table of Contents

Introduction   **5**
   Welcome to the World of Macramé   6
   What You Will Learn   8
Chapter 1: Essential Tools and Materials   **10**
   Selecting Your Cords   11
   Essential Macramé Tools   13
Chapter 2: Basic Knots and Techniques   **15**
   Learning the Core Knots   16
      The Square Knot   16
      The Spiral Knot   17
      The Half Hitch Knot   17
      The Clove Hitch   18
      The Lark's Head Knot   18
      The Diagonal Half Hitch Knot   19
      The Gathering Knot   19
      The Vertical Half Hitch Knot   20
      The Josephine Knot   20
      The Alternating Square Knot   21
      The Double Half Hitch   22
      The Vertical Clove Hitch Knot   22
      The Buttonhole Knot   23
      The Crown Knot   24
      The Picot Knot   25
   Techniques for Starting and Finishing   26
Beginner Projects   **28**
   Simple Key Chains   29
   Friendship Bracelets   31
   Basic Coasters   32
   Simple Bookmark   34
   Mini Wall Hangings   35
   Glass Jar Covers   37
   Cell Phone Pouches   39
   Sunglasses Straps   40
Home Décor Projects   **41**
   Basic Plant Hangers   42
   Simple Wall Hangings   43
   Coasters and Table Mats   46

Decorative Bottle Covers   48

Elegant Fruit Bowls   50

Chic Napkin Rings   52

Mirror Frames   54

Entryway Key and Mail Organizers   55

Functional Items   **57**

Macramé Tote Bags   58

Stylish Belts and Accessories   59

Grocery Bag Holders   61

Yoga Mat Straps   63

Camera Straps   64

Laptop Sleeves   66

Water Bottle Carriers   68

Earbud Cases   70

Modern Macramé: Innovative Projects for Beginners   **72**

Table Runners   72

Decorative Pillows and Cushions   73

Elegant Window Curtains   75

Bohemian Chic Bed Headboards   77

Luxurious Bath Mats   79

Simple Jewelry Pieces   80

Simple Macramé Room Divider   82

Detailed Chair Backings   84

Seasonal Projects   **85**

Christmas Tree Ornaments   86

Festive Garland Decorations   87

Easter Basket Enhancements   89

Halloween Themed Wall Art   91

Valentine's Day Heart Wreaths   93

Simple Thanksgiving Table Centerpieces   94

New Year's Eve Party Favors   96

Fourth of July Bunting   98

Chapter 3: Design Your Own Patterns   **99**

Principles of Pattern Design   100

Creating Custom Projects   102

Acknowledgments   **105**

Introduction

Macramé, a storied craft, invites you on a transformative journey through the interlacing of threads with history and heart. In these pages lies not just a guide to knotting but a passage to the essence of creation, a series of lessons in the art of patience, intricacy, and self-expression. You are about to immerse yourself in a practice that is both ancient and perennially new, a blend of ritual and innovation that has charmed artisans for centuries. The world of Macramé beckons with a quiet allure, promising the joy of handmade elegance and the satisfaction of crafting beauty from simplicity. Let us unfurl the cords of creativity and begin a voyage that extends far beyond the weaving of strings, into the crafting of personal narratives and connections.

Welcome to the World of Macramé

Macramé, a dance of thread and knots, a symphony of intricate patterns weaving tales as old as time—it is more than just a craft. It's a journey into the soulful depths of tradition, blended seamlessly with modern creativity. This is your invitation to step through the gateway into an art form that promises not just beauty and function but also a meditative retreat into the heart of creation itself.

In the palms of your hands, you'll cradle the silent language of cords and knots. Each twist and turn is a word, each pattern a sentence in the narrative of Macramé. Here, in the sanctuary of woven threads, you will discover the tranquil pleasure of making, the satisfaction of tactile creation that stands as a testament to both the legacy and the boundless future of this enduring craft.

Macramé's essence lies in its simplicity and the profound tranquility that comes with it. With each crossing of the cords, there's a quieting of the mind, a soothing rhythm that beckons serenity in the midst of life's clamor. This ancient form of textile-making, surprisingly relevant in the contemporary aesthetic, extends an invitation to all—regardless of age or artistic background—to engage in an act of timeless creation.

As we embark on this venture together, you'll find that Macramé is not just an art but a companion. Through the shared experiences of knotting, you will be connecting not only with the threads in your hands but also with a community, a tradition that spans across cultures and centuries. You will unravel the joy that comes from transforming humble strings into stunning pieces of handcrafted art.

This world—your new world—is not just about learning a set of skills; it's about embracing a lifestyle, a mindset. In Macramé, there's a profound appreciation for the meticulous, the gradual, and the organic. It's about the celebration of the tactile and the handmade in an era often dominated by the mass-produced and the ephemeral.

The philosophy of Macramé is anchored in patience. Like the natural world from which it draws its inspiration, it doesn't rush. It grows, evolves, and flourishes under attentive care. As you will learn, Macramé is a forgiving friend; it allows you to undo and redo until you find harmony in your creation.

In the following pages, without giving away the treasures that lie in the chapters ahead, you will begin your journey by wrapping your fingers around the core of Macramé. The foundational knots will be your building blocks, the seeds from which your garden of patterns will grow. This is where you'll learn to see potential in a pile of cords, where a plain string transforms into a vessel of creativity and expression.

Imagine, for a moment, the quiet pride of crafting something with your own hands that becomes a piece of your home, a gift for a friend, or perhaps a part of your wardrobe. There's an intimate story woven into every piece you'll create, a narrative that's uniquely yours. Macramé offers you the tools to tell that story in a language that's been spoken for centuries, yet remains as fresh and compelling as the day it was first tied and knotted.

It's important to emphasize that while the process of creating Macramé can be peaceful and introspective, it is also joyous and vibrant. The act of knotting, which at first may seem daunting, soon becomes second nature, a comfortable routine that you'll eagerly anticipate as part of your daily ritual.

We'll approach our lessons with the heart of an explorer, eager to discover not just how the knots form, but why they work the way they do. There's logic in the loops and reason in the wraps that go beyond mere aesthetics. Understanding this deeper aspect of Macramé will enhance your appreciation of the craft and expand the horizon of what you can achieve with it.

So, as you sit down with this book and your spools of cord, prepare for a voyage into a world where the ancient meets the modern, tranquility meets creativity, and simplicity meets elegance. Macramé is more than just an art—it's a dialogue with history, an embrace of the tactile, and a step into a community of makers and dreamers. Welcome, dear crafter, to the world of Macramé. Here, we begin.

What You Will Learn

Embarking on the journey of Macramé is like opening a door to a room filled with the fragrance of nostalgia, yet brimming with contemporary vibrance. As you begin this voyage with the threads of curiosity, you will weave not only the tapestries of art but also the quilt of your own growth. Here, in the cradle of your own creativity, you will learn the gentle art of patience, the steadfastness of practice, and the courage to create and let create.

Macramé does not ask for you to be an artist by trade; it simply asks you to be one in spirit. As your guide through this journey, I'll share with you the wisdom of the knot, the tales of the strings, and the quiet confidence that comes from mastering the simple to manifest the complex. What you will learn here transcends the mere ability to tie knots; it is the embodiment of process and progress.

From the moment your fingers first fumble with the cords until the day you stand back to admire the intricate web of your own making, the path is as rewarding as the destination. Through this learning experience, you will become versed in the language of lines and loops, a dialect spoken through the fingers rather than the tongue. As you traverse through these pages, a metamorphosis awaits where the seemingly inconsequential strings you hold today will transform into the foundations of your future creations.

The knowledge you will gather here is more than just practical; it is historical, emotional, and at times, philosophical. You will learn about the origins of Macramé, its journey across the oceans, and how it has become a beloved craft shared across the world. This is a testament to the human desire to create and connect, an ode to the thread that binds us to our ancestors and to each other.

Macramé teaches more than the creation of beauty; it imparts the beauty of creation. As you delve into the intricacies of knots, you will learn that each has its own purpose, its own story. The knots are but a metaphor for life's twist and turns, and you will understand how each contributes to a greater whole. You will come to appreciate the delicate balance of tension and slack, the harmony between strength and flexibility.

You will not merely learn to replicate patterns but to see the grand tapestry of possibilities within a single knot. Your hands will become skilled at speaking the silent poetry of Macramé, and your heart will find rhythm in the creation of each new piece. As your skills deepen, so too will your understanding that Macramé is not just about following a pattern—it's about forging your own.

In these lessons, there's also an unspoken wisdom, a quiet whisper that encourages you to slow down, to be present in the moment, to find joy in the meditative dance of threads. You will learn the importance of each step, the value of each knot, and the significance of each design choice. This process is about embracing imperfection as a path to uniqueness, where each 'mistake' is simply a new design waiting to be discovered.

While the beginning may seem filled with simple strings and basic knots, you are in fact laying down the roots of your Macramé journey—a journey that promises growth and an ever-evolving craft. Each chapter, each section, each paragraph you read is a stepping stone that equips you with knowledge and empowers you with technique.

Through the art of Macramé, you will learn about yourself—your patience, your precision, your persistence. You will encounter your innate ability for creativity and design, perhaps even surprising yourself with the dexterity of your own two hands. This craft will become a canvas for your personal expression, a reflection of your inner world in the form of knots and patterns.

As your journey unfolds, you will realize that learning Macramé is not a solitary pursuit but a communal experience. You will become part of a lineage of crafters, each with their own story, each knot a stitch in the fabric of a shared history. You will learn from the past, create in the present, and inspire the future.

Macramé is about connection—to the self, to the material, to the community. As you learn the knots, create patterns, and complete projects, you will find yourself part of a larger conversation, one that speaks of the importance of handcrafted art in our lives. You will learn the language of Macramé, yes, but more importantly, you will learn its heart, its pulse, and its boundless potential to bring beauty into the world.

And so, with threads in hand and a spirit eager for adventure, you are ready to begin. Welcome to the world of Macramé—a world where every knot counts, where every pattern tells a story, and where you, dear crafter, are the narrator.

Chapter 1: Essential Tools and Materials

The alchemy of Macramé begins not with a flamboyant flourish of activity, but with the quiet selection of cords and the gentle assembly of tools. These first steps are akin to setting the stage for a performance, where each element plays a crucial role in the success of the show. The materials and tools are the unsung foundation of every knot and weave, the bedrock upon which the tapestry of this timeless craft will unfold. As you acquaint yourself with these essential elements, you embark on a path that is as much about preparation as it is about the act of creation itself.

Selecting Your Cords

At the heart of every Macramé piece, from the smallest woven bracelet to the grandest hanging tapestry, lies a singular, unassuming hero: the cord. It is both the foundation and the medium of your craft, a humble actor ready to take the stage in the theater of knotting. When you select your cords, you're not just choosing a tool; you're deciding on the texture of your art, the palette of your creativity, and the very substance of your designs.

To choose a cord is to understand the soul of Macramé. There's a dialogue that begins here, between the artisan and the thread, a conversation that will influence every aspect of your crafting journey. The cords you choose are not merely strands to be tied; they are whispers of potential, awaiting the touch of your hands to be shaped into expressions of your innermost artistic visions.

The selection process is an art form in itself, one that requires consideration of material, size, color, and flexibility. As you navigate through the sea of options, you will learn to listen with your fingers, to find the cord that speaks to your sense of touch, and resonates with your creative spirit. The cords are your companions on this odyssey, and like any good companion, they must be chosen with care and thoughtfulness.

Imagine the cotton cord, soft and pliable, with its promise of gentle curves and a forgiving nature, ideal for the delicate dance of the basic knots. It is here, with cotton, that many begin their journey, finding comfort in its versatility and its kind embrace of both novice and skilled hands alike. Or consider the jute, earthy and robust, evoking the spirit of nature with its raw texture and sturdy composition, a perfect match for those yearning to echo the aesthetics of the natural world.

The choice of cord can influence not just the appearance but also the feel of your creations. The supple touch of a silk blend cord can add a hint of luxury to your work, a whisper of elegance that elevates the simplest design. In contrast, the steadfastness of nylon speaks to durability and boldness, offering a vivid array of colors that can stand the test of sunlight and time.

Yet, selection goes beyond the tactile and visual; it's about foreseeing the interaction of cord and knot. It's about anticipating the drape of a wall hanging or the sturdiness of a plant hanger. Your cords must align with your intentions, must carry the weight of your aspirations, and hold the promise of your envisioned masterpiece. The correct cord can transform a basic knot into a statement, a simple design into a work of art.

Your cord selection becomes a testament to your personal style and your projected designs. Will you choose a monochrome palette to emphasize form and shadow, or will you delve into the vibrant hues that speak the language of vivacity and joy? Each color you choose weaves its own story, sets its own mood, and creates its own impact.

As you hold the cord in your hands, think of the shapes it will form, the weight it will carry, the space it will occupy. You are not merely selecting a cord; you are casting the lead actor in your upcoming piece. This decision, seemingly simple, is laden with the depth of your forthcoming creative endeavors.

And when you find that perfect cord, when it sits snugly in the palm of your hand, as if it was meant to be there, you will understand that the process of selection was not just about the cord. It was about setting the stage for creativity, about preparing to breathe life into your ideas. It was about finding the thread that connects your vision to reality, the thread that will soon become an extension of your own fingers as you begin the rhythmic dance of knotting.

In this exploration of cords, let examples serve not as strict guides but as inspiration. Consider the intricate beauty of a fine cord used to create a delicate piece of jewelry, or the strength and resilience of a thicker one that forms the backbone of a sturdy tote bag. Each example is a lesson in suitability, in understanding that the cord is not just a means but an integral part of the final creation.

So, as you stand at this crossroad, ready to choose the cords that will carry your Macramé journey forward, remember that this is where it all begins. This is where your craft takes root, where your project starts to take shape in your mind's eye. Choose wisely, choose boldly, and let your selection be the first stroke of brilliance on the canvas of your Macramé adventure.

Essential Macramé Tools

The artist's studio is a sanctuary, a space where creativity is conjured and brought to life. In the world of Macramé, this studio is not defined by four walls but by the tools that make the craft possible. With the cords chosen, your next step into the sanctum of Macramé is to gather the tools that will turn possibility into reality.

The tools of Macramé are humble, yet they hold within them the power to transform. They are the silent partners in your creative process, the unsung heroes that work in the shadow of the cords. A Macramé tool is an extension of your hand, it must feel right, as if it was made for you, and you alone. These tools will be your constant companions, the bearers of your craft, the instruments through which your artistry will flow.

First, consider the dowel, rod, or ring that serves as the backbone of your piece. These are the sentinels, the steadfast pillars upon which your Macramé will come to life. They must be chosen for strength and for the harmony they will share with the cords. They are the silent foundation, the unshakable frame upon which your tapestry of knots will drape.

Next, the cutting tool, perhaps a pair of scissors or shears, is your sculptor's chisel. It must be sharp, precise, and comfortable in your hand. With each snip, it defines the borders of your creation, cutting away the excess, leaving behind only what is meant to be a part of the final piece. Your cutting tool is not merely a blade; it is the executor of decisions, the finisher of ends, the definer of boundaries.

The measuring tape is your navigator, guiding you through lengths and widths, ensuring that your creation is not led astray by guesswork. It is a simple tool, yet its role is critical, ensuring that symmetry and proportion are maintained, and that your work is true to your vision.

The brush, though not often spoken of, plays its part in the final presentation. It is the groomer of your work, coaxing out every tassel, straightening every fringe, ensuring that each piece is not just made but presented with the utmost care and intention. The brush is the polisher of the final image, the tool that preens the rough edges into smooth cascades of fiber.

Hooks and needles, though small, are the connectors, the tools that bring pieces together, that add embellishments and join sections. They must be sturdy yet deft, capable of working with precision, threading beads or combining segments into a cohesive whole. They are the quiet diplomats, marrying different elements of your work into a unified presentation.

In this discussion of tools, one might imagine a craftsman's belt, laden with gadgets and gizmos, but such is not the case. Macramé asks for little but requires that little to be of the best, of the highest compatibility with the artist.

For instance, the work of a Macramé artist creating a wall hanging would be incomplete without mentioning the board to which their piece is pinned. This board is a stage, allowing each cord to be placed, adjusted, and knotted with precision. The pins that hold the cords are like quiet sentries, ensuring that everything stays in place, providing tension and holding patterns steady as the artist weaves their spell of knots.

Each tool is chosen not just for its function but for the feel, the comfort, the way it fits into the flow of work. The tools must not interrupt the artist's rhythm; they should be so natural in their use that they become invisible, allowing the mind to focus purely on the act of creation.

In these early stages of your Macramé journey, the tools you choose will become familiar, like the touch of an old friend. They will bear witness to your growth as an artist, from the first tentative knot to the confident sweep of patterns that will later emerge.

The importance of each tool cannot be overstated, for they collectively represent the tactile experience of Macramé. They are the conduits of your creativity, the tangible links between your artistic vision and the physical manifestation of that vision.

So, gather your tools with the same care that you selected your cords. Hold them, feel them, and understand that they are more than just objects; they are the facilitators of your craft, the silent supporters of your art. With these tools in hand, your studio, your sanctuary of Macramé, is complete, and you are ready to embark on the noble task of creating beauty from the simplest of beginnings.

Chapter 2: Basic Knots and Techniques

Embark upon the fundamental voyage into the essence of Macramé, where the timeless dance of knots becomes a testament to the artistry of hands. The symphony of basic knots and techniques is a ballet of intricacy and strength, a precise language that breathes life into the cords. Within this realm, each knot is a narrative, and every technique is a chapter in the story you're about to weave. The fluency gained here is the bedrock of all future creations, the silent beats to which all Macramé artisans sway.

Learning the Core Knots

Within the realm of Macramé, knots are the lexicon, the fundamental expressions through which all designs speak. They are the basic units, the alphabets that combine to form the language of this craft. To learn these core knots is to begin to understand the dialogue between the fibers that pass through your fingers. It is here, in the mastery of these basic elements, that the journey from novice to artisan truly begins.

When you first encounter the core knots, you approach them not merely as techniques to be memorized, but as individual characters to be known, understood, and befriended. These knots carry stories within their loops and turns, and as you practice them, you will find that they begin to reveal the secrets of their construction, the logic behind their function, and the beauty within their form.

The Square Knot

The square knot is perhaps the most fundamental of Macramé knots. It is reliable, versatile, and foundational. In its symmetry lies balance, and in its repetition, a rhythm that can become meditative. As you loop the cords, first left over right, then right over left, you create the heartbeat of many Macramé pieces. The square knot is your steady companion, the one that will appear time and again, a familiar presence in the tapestry of your crafting adventures.

Instructions:

1. Start with two cords (A and B) folded in half, creating four strands.
2. Take the left cord (A1) and cross it over the two middle cords (A2 and B2), and under the right cord (B1).

3. Take the right cord (B1), cross it under the two middle cords (A2 and B2), and over the left cord (A1).

4. Pull both ends to tighten the knot.

5. Repeat the process, this time starting with the right cord (B1) over the middle cords (A2 and B2), and under the left cord (A1).

6. Pull both ends to complete the square knot.

The Spiral Knot

The spiral knot, a variant of the square knot, introduces movement and energy into your work. It twirls and spins, creating a helix that adds texture and dimension. The spiral knot is the dance of Macramé, a reminder that within the structure of this craft, there is also freedom and grace. As you alternate the knots one-sidedly, you will see the birth of a twist, an echo of the spirals found in seashells and galaxies.

Instructions:

1. Start with two cords (A and B) folded in half, creating four strands.

2. Take the left cord (A1) and cross it over the two middle cords (A2 and B2), and under the right cord (B1).

3. Take the right cord (B1), cross it under the two middle cords (A2 and B2), and over the left cord (A1).

4. Pull both ends to tighten the knot.

5. Repeat the process, always starting with the same side (left or right). This repetition will create a spiral effect.

The Half Hitch Knot

The half hitch knot introduces direction and narrative, guiding lines along paths that can curve, twist, and turn. It is a knot that asks for your focus, for your hands to become confident in leading the cords with intention. As you loop and pull, you'll find that the half hitch can form patterns and borders, become a supporting structure for more complex designs, or stand alone in its simplicity.

Instructions:

1. Start with two cords: one working cord (A) and one holding cord (B).

2. Place the working cord (A) over the holding cord (B), creating a loop.

3. Pull the working cord (A) through the loop created and tighten.
4. Repeat the process along the holding cord (B) to create a series of half hitch knots.

The Clove Hitch

The clove hitch, similar in nature but distinct in purpose, is a knot of anchors and beginnings. It is where strands can be added, where new stories can start on the warp of your Macramé piece. This knot requires precision, a gentle tension that holds firm yet does not constrict. It is the breath in-between, the space where one chapter ends and another begins.

Instructions:

1. Start with the working cord (A) and the holding cord (B).
2. Wrap the working cord (A) over and around the holding cord (B) to form a loop.
3. Pass the working cord (A) over itself and under the holding cord (B) to form a second loop.
4. Tighten the knot by pulling both ends of the working cord (A).

The Lark's Head Knot

The Lark's Head Knot, also known as the Cow Hitch, is one of the simplest and most fundamental knots in macramé. It is often used to attach cords to a support, such as a ring or a dowel, and forms the basis for many other knots and projects. The Lark's Head Knot symbolizes stability and beginning, allowing the cords to be securely anchored and ready for creation.

Instructions:

1. **Preparation**: Take the cord and fold it in half, creating a loop at the center.
2. **Positioning**: Hold the support (a ring, dowel, or rod) in front of you.
3. **Inserting the Loop**: Pass the loop of the cord over the support, leaving the loop free in front.
4. **Completing the Knot**: Take the ends of the cord (the two free parts) and thread them through the loop that you passed over the support.
5. **Tightening**: Pull the ends of the cord downward to tighten the knot. Make sure the knot is secure and centered on the support.

The Diagonal Half Hitch Knot

The Diagonal Half Hitch Knot is a versatile knot that adds direction and texture to your macramé work. It is often used to create diagonal lines and patterns, adding a sense of movement and flow to your designs. This knot is essential for creating intricate and structured macramé pieces.

Instructions:
1. **Preparation**: Choose a holding cord (A) and a working cord (B). The holding cord will remain straight, while the working cord will create the knot.
2. **Positioning**: Hold the holding cord (A) diagonally across your work area.
3. **First Half Hitch**: Take the working cord (B) and pass it over the holding cord (A), then bring it under the holding cord, creating a loop.
4. **Tightening**: Pull the working cord (B) through the loop you just created, tightening it to form the first half hitch.
5. **Second Half Hitch**: Repeat the process by passing the working cord (B) over the holding cord (A) again, bringing it under and through the loop, then tightening it.
6. **Continuation**: Continue adding half hitches along the holding cord (A), maintaining a diagonal direction.

The Gathering Knot

The Gathering Knot, also known as the Wrapping Knot, is a useful and decorative knot that is often used to secure multiple cords together or to finish off the ends of macramé pieces. It provides a clean and polished look, making it ideal for creating tassels or adding a neat finish to your work.

Instructions:
1. **Preparation**: Gather the cords you want to secure and hold them together in a bundle.
2. **Positioning**: Take a separate piece of cord (the working cord) and lay it parallel to the bundle, leaving a short tail.
3. **Creating the Loop**: Form a small loop with the working cord, placing the loop downward along the bundle.
4. **Wrapping**: Start wrapping the working cord around the bundle and the loop, working your way downward. Wrap tightly and neatly, covering the loop.

5. **Securing the Knot**: Once you have made several wraps, take the end of the working cord and thread it through the loop at the bottom.

6. **Tightening**: Hold the end of the working cord and pull the short tail at the top. This will pull the loop and the end of the working cord inside the wraps, securing the knot.

7. **Trimming**: Trim any excess cord ends to create a clean finish.

The Vertical Half Hitch Knot

The Vertical Half Hitch Knot is a versatile knot that adds vertical lines and texture to your macramé work. It is often used to create vertical patterns, adding structure and design to your pieces. This knot is essential for creating detailed and organized macramé designs.

Instructions:

1. **Preparation**: Choose a holding cord (A) and a working cord (B). The holding cord will remain vertical, while the working cord will create the knot.

2. **Positioning**: Hold the holding cord (A) vertically in your work area.

3. **First Half Hitch**: Take the working cord (B) and pass it over the holding cord (A), then bring it under the holding cord, creating a loop.

4. **Tightening**: Pull the working cord (B) through the loop you just created, tightening it to form the first half hitch.

5. **Second Half Hitch**: Repeat the process by passing the working cord (B) over the holding cord (A) again, bringing it under and through the loop, then tightening it.

6. **Continuation**: Continue adding half hitches along the holding cord (A), maintaining a vertical direction.

The Josephine Knot

The Josephine Knot, a variation of the Lover's Knot, is a decorative and intricate knot that adds an elegant touch to your macramé projects. This knot forms a beautiful looping pattern that is perfect for adding visual interest and complexity to your designs.

Instructions:

1. **Preparation**: Choose two cords (A and B) that you want to use to form the knot.

2. **Creating the Loop**: Form a loop with cord A by crossing it over itself, creating a circle.

3. **Positioning the Second Cord**: Take cord B and weave it under the loop formed by cord A.

4. **Weaving Cord B**: Bring cord B over the top of the loop and then under the end of cord A.

5. **Continuing the Weave**: Pull cord B over itself and then weave it back under the loop of cord A.

6. **Final Adjustments**: Adjust the knot by carefully pulling the ends of both cords to tighten and shape the Josephine Knot.

The Alternating Square Knot

The Alternating Square Knot is a fundamental knot in macramé that creates a beautiful, woven pattern. By alternating the square knots, you can create a sturdy and visually appealing design that is perfect for a variety of projects, from plant hangers to wall hangings.

Instructions:

1. **Preparation**: Choose four cords (A, B, C, and D) to work with. Arrange them in a straight line with A and D as the outer cords and B and C as the inner cords.

2. **First Square Knot**:
   1. Take cord A (left outer cord) and place it over cords B and C (middle cords), then under cord D (right outer cord).
   2. Take cord D and place it under cords B and C, then pull it through the loop formed by cord A.
   3. Pull both outer cords (A and D) to tighten the knot.
   4. Repeat this process, but start with the right outer cord (D) over the middle cords and under the left outer cord (A). Then, pull the left outer cord (A) under the middle cords and through the loop formed by cord D.
   5. Tighten the knot to complete the first square knot.

3. **Alternating the Knots**:
   1. Skip the first and last cords (A and D) and use the next four cords (B, C, E, and F) to make the next square knot, following the same steps as above.
   2. After completing the second square knot, return to the original cords (A, B, C, and D) and make another square knot, but shift one cord to the left or right, depending on your pattern.

4. **Continuation**: Continue alternating the square knots in this manner, ensuring each new row shifts the cords to create the alternating pattern.

The Double Half Hitch

The Double Half Hitch Knot is a versatile and essential knot in macramé that is used to create lines, curves, and intricate patterns. By using this knot, you can add both structure and decorative elements to your macramé projects.

Instructions:

1. **Preparation**: Choose a holding cord (A) and a working cord (B). The holding cord will remain taut, while the working cord will create the knots.
2. **First Half Hitch**:
   1. Hold the holding cord (A) horizontally or diagonally, depending on the desired direction of the knot.
   2. Take the working cord (B) and pass it over the holding cord (A), then under the holding cord, creating a loop.
   3. Pull the working cord (B) through the loop, tightening it to form the first half hitch.
3. **Second Half Hitch**:
   1. With the same working cord (B), pass it over the holding cord (A) again, creating a second loop.
   2. Pull the working cord (B) through this second loop and tighten it to secure the second half hitch.
4. **Continuation**: Repeat the process along the holding cord, creating a series of double half hitches to form a line or pattern.

The Vertical Clove Hitch Knot

The Vertical Clove Hitch Knot is a fundamental knot in macramé that is used to create vertical lines and patterns. This knot adds structure and texture to your designs, making it ideal for creating detailed and organized macramé pieces.

Instructions:

1. **Preparation**: Choose a holding cord (A) and a working cord (B). The holding cord will remain vertical, while the working cord will create the knots.
2. **First Hitch**:
   1. Hold the holding cord (A) vertically in your work area.
   2. Take the working cord (B) and pass it over the holding cord (A), creating a loop.
   3. Bring the working cord (B) under the holding cord (A) and pull it through the loop, tightening it to form the first half hitch.
3. **Second Hitch**:
   1. With the same working cord (B), pass it over the holding cord (A) again, but this time start below the first hitch.
   2. Bring the working cord (B) under the holding cord (A) and pull it through the loop, tightening it to secure the second half hitch.
4. **Continuation**: Repeat the process along the holding cord, creating a series of vertical clove hitches to form a line or pattern.

The Buttonhole Knot

The Buttonhole Knot is a practical and decorative knot used for creating closures in macramé projects, such as bracelets or bags. This knot forms a loop that can be used as a buttonhole, providing a secure and functional closure for your designs.

Instructions:

1. **Preparation**: Choose a cord (A) to form the buttonhole knot. Ensure the cord is long enough to create a loop and secure the knot.
2. **Creating the Loop**:
   1. Fold the cord (A) to create a loop of the desired size for the buttonhole.
   2. Hold the loop in place with one hand, ensuring the loop's ends are even.
3. **Forming the Knot**:
   1. With the ends of the cord (A), create a simple overhand knot by crossing the ends over each other and pulling them through the loop created by the crossing cords.
   2. Tighten the overhand knot around the base of the loop, ensuring the loop remains the desired size.

4. **Securing the Knot**:
    1. For additional security, you can tie a second overhand knot using the ends of the cord (A) just below the first knot.
    2. Pull the knots tightly to secure the loop in place.
5. **Trimming**: Trim any excess cord ends to create a clean finish.

The Crown Knot

The Crown Knot is a decorative and functional knot often used in macramé to create a rounded finish or to add ornamental detail. This knot is perfect for adding texture and visual interest to your macramé projects.

Instructions:

1. **Preparation**: Choose four cords (A, B, C, and D) of equal length. Arrange them in a cross shape, with each cord pointing in a different direction (north, south, east, and west).
2. **First Loop**:
    1. Take cord A (north) and fold it over to the right, laying it parallel to cord D (east).
3. **Second Loop**:
    1. Take cord D (east) and fold it down over cord A, laying it parallel to cord C (south).
4. **Third Loop**:
    1. Take cord C (south) and fold it to the left over cord D, laying it parallel to cord B (west).
5. **Fourth Loop**:
    1. Take cord B (west) and fold it up over cord C. Then, tuck it under the loop created by cord A.
6. **Tightening the Knot**:
    1. Carefully pull all four ends of the cords to tighten the knot evenly.
7. **Continuation**: For a more intricate design, you can continue adding crown knots by repeating the steps with the same cords.

The Picot Knot

The Picot Knot is a decorative knot used in macramé to create small loops or "picots" along the edge of a pattern. These loops add texture and a delicate, ornamental touch to your macramé projects.

Instructions:

1. **Preparation**: Choose the cords you will use to create the picot knot. Typically, the picot knot is made using a working cord (A) and a base cord (B).
2. **Creating the Loop**:
   1. Determine where you want to place the picot. Hold the base cord (B) taut.
   2. Take the working cord (A) and make a small loop by folding it over itself.
3. **Forming the Knot**:
   1. With the loop in place, wrap the working cord (A) around the base cord (B) and pull it through the loop you created.
   2. Adjust the size of the loop (picot) to your desired length.
4. **Securing the Knot**:
   1. Tighten the working cord (A) to secure the picot in place. Make sure the loop remains the size you want as you pull the knot tight.
5. **Continuation**: Continue creating picot knots along the base cord as desired, spacing them evenly for a consistent look.

By mastering these knots, you will have the foundation to create a wide variety of Macramé projects. Practice each one carefully, and soon you'll be able to combine them into intricate and beautiful designs.

As you practice these knots, your hands will learn their shapes and idiosyncrasies, the way they look and feel under tension and in rest. You will come to understand that the consistency of your knots gives rise to the even texture of your work, the regularity that allows patterns to emerge and designs to take form. Each knot tied is a step further along your path, a mark of progress in the language of Macramé.

Learning these core knots is more than just a mechanical memorization—it is an immersive experience. It is where intuition begins to build, where you start to anticipate the flow of the cords, and where your hands begin to move with the certainty of knowledge. With each repetition, the motions become more natural, the knots more consistent, and your confidence grows.

As you journey through the landscape of these core knots, you will discover that they are the building blocks for all that is to come. They are the roots from which the intricate beauty of Macramé grows. Each square knot, each spiral turn, each half hitch and clove hitch is a step on a ladder, ascending towards the heights of your creative potential.

This learning is not just about tying knots; it is about cultivating a relationship with the medium of your craft. It is about finding your rhythm within the weave and flow of the cords. These knots are your first words in a new language, the beginnings of a conversation with Macramé that will grow richer and more nuanced with time.

So, approach these core knots with patience and with respect, for they are the venerable teachers that will impart upon you the first wisdom of the craft. Practice them with diligence and with care, knowing that each twist and tuck is a note in the symphony of your developing skill. In learning these knots, you are laying the foundation upon which all your future Macramé creations will stand.

Techniques for Starting and Finishing

Every artist knows that a piece of art is not just about the colors splashed across a canvas or the chiseled shape of a sculpture. It's about the beginnings and the ends, the first brushstroke and the final touch, that together encapsulate the essence of the creation. In Macramé, the initiation and culmination of your work are just as paramount as the intricate web of knots that lie between. These techniques for starting and finishing not only provide a structural framework but also reflect the thoughtfulness and integrity of the maker.

Starting a Macramé piece is to stand at the precipice of creation, poised to step into a realm of limitless potential. Your starting technique is the opening sentence of your story, the first chord in the melody you're about to weave. Whether you begin with a lark's head knot that affixes your cord to the dowel with the promise of stability and ease, or you venture into the world of mounting knots, offering a more decorative commencement, your choice sets the tone for your piece.

Imagine your cords, arrayed like the opening notes of a symphony, each one a silent participant, awaiting your cue. The lark's head, with its folded middle draped over the rod and pulled through itself, offers an embrace, a gentle grip that assures security. It's a knot that speaks of beginnings, of the basic gesture of attaching, of being poised to launch into the rhythm of creation.

But beyond the security of the lark's head, you might choose a gathering knot, a conclave of strings cinched together by a single binder cord, creating a tassel-like start that whispers of intricacy and group harmony. Here, your work starts with a gathering, a community of cords bound by a single purpose, ready to unfold into the narrative you wish to tell.

The way you start is as important as the path you choose to travel. Your starting knots are the roots from which the strength of your piece will draw. They are the anchors that hold fast against the pull and tug of your creative process. They embody the intention with which you approach your craft—a quiet yet definitive statement of the commitment you make to each piece.

And as you journey through the creation, adding knots, layering patterns, and infusing your work with your own unique voice, you will eventually arrive at the end. Finishing a Macramé piece is not just a conclusion; it is the final stanza of your poem, the closing scene of your play. It is a moment that calls for celebration, reflection, and meticulous care.

The techniques for finishing are as varied as the starts, each with its own language and story. The seamless overhand knot, which can tuck away the loose ends, is a popular choice. It is a finale that speaks to simplicity and neatness, a quiet endnote that doesn't overshadow the complexity of your work but instead seals it with quiet confidence.

Or perhaps you'll opt for the flamboyance of fringes, allowing the cords to cascade freely, giving them the freedom to dance with the movements of the air. Here, the finish is a celebration, an exuberant release, an expression of joy that reverberates with the movements of life.

For some, the end comes in the form of intricate beadwork, where the final knot is hidden behind the luster of a bead, a jeweled punctuation that adorns the termination point with an air of elegance and mystery. Here, the finish is a secret, a treasure nestled within the folds of your piece.

And yet, there are times when the best finish is one that allows for continuity, a seamless transition that hints at ongoing stories, at tales yet to be told. Techniques such as the adjustable closing, where knots can slide and adjust, bring an element of interaction and transformation, allowing your Macramé to evolve even after the final knot is tied.

Your finishing technique is the signature at the bottom of your canvas, the maker's mark that says, "This piece is complete." It's a declaration of fulfillment, a moment to stand back and appreciate the journey from the first knot to the last. It's an assertion of pride and accomplishment, a signal to the world that what was once a collection of cords is now a crafted piece of art, ready to be shared, displayed, and admired.

Starting and finishing in Macramé are about honoring the process, about understanding that each piece is a cycle, a complete experience from inception to realization. These techniques are the bookends of your creation, holding within them every knot, every choice, and every moment of inspiration that occurred between their execution. As you master these techniques, you learn not just the mechanics but the poetry of starting and finishing, the art of opening and closing the sacred space of creation.

Beginner Projects

Simple Key Chains

Project Goal:

The aim is to create a functional and stylish key chain using basic Macramé knots. This project is perfect for beginners looking to get started with Macramé while producing a useful item that can be used daily or given as a thoughtful handmade gift.

Materials Needed:

- Cotton cord: 3mm thickness, about 30 inches per keychain
- Key ring: 1-inch diameter
- Scissors
- Measuring tape

Knot Techniques Used:

- Lark's Head Knot
- Square Knots
- Spiral Knots (optional)

Procedure:

Preparation of Materials:

1. Cut the cotton cord into four 30-inch lengths.
2. Fold each piece of cord in half to double it and create a loop at the fold.

Beginning the Work:

1. Attach the cords to the key ring using a Lark's Head Knot. To do this, pass the loop of the folded cord through the key ring, then pull the cord ends through the loop and tighten to secure them to the ring.

Project Development:

1. Start by arranging the cords so they lay flat. You will have eight strands hanging from the key ring.
2. Begin tying Square Knots using the four middle strands as the base and the outer strands to tie the knots. Continue tying square knots to create a band about 2 inches long.
3. Optionally, switch to Spiral Knots for an additional inch to add a decorative twist to the keychain.
4. Make sure all knots are tight and even to ensure a uniform appearance.

Assembly and Finishing:

1. Once the desired length of knots is completed, finish off with an overhand knot using all the strands to secure the end.
2. Trim the excess cord to create a neat tassel at the end of the key chain.
3. Optionally, you can apply a small amount of clear glue to the ends of the cords to prevent fraying.

Helpful Hints:

- Maintaining even tension on the cords while knotting is crucial for a uniform appearance.
- Choose a soft, flexible cord to make knotting easier and the final product more appealing.
- Experiment with different colors of cords to personalize or match different styles.

Expected Result: The finished product should be a stylish and sturdy Macramé key chain with a solid band of neatly arranged knots, topped with a tidy tassel. The key chain should be functional, adding a touch of handmade charm to everyday items like keys.

Friendship Bracelets

Project Goal:

The goal is to create a set of colorful friendship bracelets using basic macramé techniques. This project allows beginners to practice precise knotting while producing wearable art that symbolizes friendship and can be shared among friends.

Materials Needed:

- Embroidery floss or thin cotton yarn in various colors
- Scissors
- Tape or a clipboard to secure the bracelet while working
- Measuring tape

Knot Techniques Used:

- Square Knot
- Diagonal Half Hitch

Procedure:

Preparation of Materials:

1. Choose several colors of embroidery floss or cotton yarn. Cut each color into strands about 60 inches long, depending on the desired length of the bracelet.
2. Gather all strands together, fold them in half to create a loop at the fold point, and knot them to form a starting loop. Leave a small loop through which the bracelet can be fastened later.

Beginning the Work:

1. Secure the loop under a clipboard or tape it to a table to keep the bracelet steady while you work.
2. Arrange the strands by color in the order you want them to appear in the bracelet.

Project Development:

1. Start with the outermost strand on the left side and make a series of diagonal half hitch knots across all the other strands, moving from left to right. This will create a diagonal stripe across the bracelet.
2. Repeat this process with the next outermost strand, continuing until you have reached the desired length of the bracelet.
3. Throughout the process, alternate the direction of the diagonal half hitch to create a zigzag or a straight diagonal pattern based on your preference.

4. Use square knots intermittently to add variation or to create sections of different textures within the bracelet.

Assembly and Finishing:

1. Once the desired length is reached, tie all the strands together in an overhand knot to secure the end of the bracelet.
2. Trim the excess strands to create a neat finish.
3. The bracelet can be fastened by tying the end strands through the loop created at the beginning.

Helpful Hints:

- Keep the tension consistent in your knots to ensure the bracelet forms evenly and lies flat when worn.
- Mixing colors and adjusting the sequence of knotting can create unique patterns and personalize each bracelet.
- Consider adding beads or small charms to the strands before knotting for an extra decorative touch.

Expected Result: The finished friendship bracelets should be vibrant and evenly knotted, featuring smooth diagonal lines or zigzag patterns. They should fit comfortably around the wrist, with a secure knot and clean finishing. These bracelets are ideal as gifts or as a group craft activity, providing a wearable reminder of shared bonds.

Basic Coasters

Project Goal:

This project aims to create a set of functional and aesthetically pleasing coasters using basic Macramé knots. Ideal for beginners, these coasters will protect surfaces while adding a touch of handmade charm to any home decor.

Materials Needed:

- Cotton cord, 4mm thickness, approximately 10 feet per coaster
- Scissors
- Measuring tape
- A comb or brush for fringing (optional)

Knot Techniques Used:

- Spiral Knot
- Square Knot

Procedure:

Preparation of Materials:

1. Cut the cotton cord into 10-foot lengths, one for each coaster you plan to make.
2. Fold each length in half to find the center and create a loop at this midpoint.

Beginning the Work:

1. Create a loop at the center of the cord using a Lark's Head Knot. This will serve as the starting point for your coaster.
2. Secure the loop to a flat work surface using tape or a heavy object to keep it in place during knotting.

Project Development:

1. Divide the strands into four groups of two (if using the standard 4mm cord). Begin working with one group, tying a series of square knots to create a straight edge starting from the looped center.
2. Continue with adjacent groups, ensuring each segment is tightly knotted to form a cohesive pattern. Use spiral knots for a decorative effect, rotating around the initial center loop.
3. Expand the coaster outward by continuously adding square knots around the existing knots, building out in a circular or square shape, depending on your design preference.
4. Ensure each round of knots is snug and evenly spaced to maintain the coaster's shape and flatness.

Assembly and Finishing:

1. Once the coaster has reached the desired size (typically about 4-5 inches in diameter for circular coasters or side length for square coasters), finish by tying a final row of tight square knots.
2. Cut off the excess cord, leaving about an inch and a half for a fringe, if desired. Use a comb or brush to unravel these ends, creating a soft edge.
3. Trim the fringe evenly to ensure a tidy and uniform look.

Helpful Hints:

- Regularly adjust and tighten knots from the center outwards to prevent the coaster from cupping or becoming uneven.
- Use a flat, heat-resistant surface under your work area to press the coaster flat periodically throughout the knotting process.
- Consider using waterproofing spray on the finished coasters to protect them from moisture and stains, especially if using lighter-colored cords.

Expected Result: The finished coasters should be robust and lay flat against any surface, with a uniform pattern and neat fringes (if applied). They will provide a practical yet decorative element to coffee tables, dining tables, or desks, reflecting the craftsmanship and care put into their creation. Each coaster should be able to withstand regular use, offering a durable and stylish option for home use or as a gift.

Simple Bookmark

Project Goal:

The goal of this project is to create a simple, elegant bookmark using basic Macramé techniques. This beginner-friendly project will provide a practical and charming accessory for any book lover, combining functionality with the artistry of handmade craft.

Materials Needed:

- Cotton or hemp cord, 2mm thickness, approximately 24 inches per bookmark
- Scissors
- Measuring tape
- Optional: beads or charms for decoration
- Optional: a small comb for fringing

Knot Techniques Used:

- Square Knot
- Diagonal Half Hitch

Procedure:

Preparation of Materials:

1. Cut the cord into a 24-inch length.
2. Fold the cord in half to create a central loop at the top, which will also serve as the top of the bookmark.

Beginning the Work:

1. Start by securing the loop under a clipboard or with a piece of tape on a flat surface to keep it stable.
2. Arrange the cords so they lay flat and are easy to work with.

Project Development:

1. Begin by tying square knots to form the main body of the bookmark. Continue making square knots to create a band that is approximately 6 inches long.

2. Switch to diagonal half hitch knots for a more textured, decorative border. Using one of the outer cords as a guide, tie diagonal half hitches around it with the other cord.

3. Continue this pattern around both sides of the bookmark to create a symmetric, decorative edge.

4. Optionally, incorporate beads or charms into the design by threading them onto the cord before tying knots to secure them in place.

Assembly and Finishing:

1. Once you reach the desired length, complete the bookmark with a final square knot to ensure all elements are securely tied.

2. Cut any excess cord below the final knot, leaving about 2 inches if you wish to add a fringed end.

3. If a fringe is desired, unravel the remaining cord ends with a small comb to create a soft, decorative finish.

4. Trim the fringe to ensure it is even and tidy.

Helpful Hints:

- Ensure all knots are tied with consistent tension to keep the bookmark flat and uniform.
- If using beads, choose ones with holes large enough to fit the thickness of the cord but secure enough not to move freely once in place.
- Consider using a stiffer cord or applying a light fabric stiffener to the finished bookmark to ensure it holds its shape and stays in place inside books.

Expected Result: The finished bookmark should be sleek and functional, with a neatly knotted body and an attractively textured edge. It should slide easily into a book but be sturdy enough to handle frequent use. If beads or charms are added, they should complement the design and add a personal touch without overwhelming the bookmark's simplicity. This Macramé bookmark is not only a practical tool for readers but also a wonderful gift idea or a small personal project that adds a touch of handmade artistry to everyday life.

Mini Wall Hangings

Project Goal:

The aim is to create a mini wall hanging, a perfect project for beginners looking to introduce a decorative touch to their home or workspace. This project allows individuals to explore the basics of Macramé while creating a piece that adds warmth and texture to small spaces.

Materials Needed:

- Cotton or hemp cord, 3mm thickness, approximately 50 inches per hanging
- A small wooden dowel or stick, 6 to 8 inches in length
- Scissors
- Measuring tape
- Optional: beads or small decorative items for embellishment

Knot Techniques Used:

- Lark's Head Knot
- Square Knot
- Spiral Knot

Procedure:

Preparation of Materials:

1. Cut four pieces of cord, each measuring 50 inches in length.
2. If adding beads or decorations, prepare these by ensuring they fit the cord and are ready to be threaded.

Beginning the Work:

1. Fold each piece of cord in half and attach it to the wooden dowel using the Lark's Head Knot. You will have eight strands hanging from the dowel once all cords are attached.
2. Secure the dowel to a flat working surface with tape or by hanging it from a hook to maintain stability while working.

Project Development:

1. Begin by tying a row of Square Knots using the eight strands. Group the strands into pairs, using the outer strands to tie the knots around the inner strands.
2. After completing a row of Square Knots, proceed with a few Spiral Knots for added texture and visual interest. Create the Spiral Knots by continuing to tie Square Knots but only twisting in one direction.
3. Continue alternating between a few rows of Square Knots and sections of Spiral Knots, creating a patterned texture. Feel free to experiment with the length and frequency of each knot type to create a unique design.
4. Optionally, incorporate beads by threading them onto one or more of the cords before continuing with additional knots, securing the beads in place.

Assembly and Finishing:

1. Once the desired length and design are achieved (usually around 10-15 inches long), finish the piece by tying a horizontal row of Square Knots at the bottom to ensure all cords are securely tied off.
2. Trim the excess cord below this final row to create a neat fringe. Comb out the fringe with a fine-tooth comb or brush if a softer look is desired.
3. If used, make sure all beads or decorations are securely in place and adjust as necessary to enhance the overall look.

Helpful Hints:

- Maintain even tension and consistent spacing with all knots to ensure the wall hanging hangs straight and looks uniform.
- Customize the color of the cords or add multiple colors to create vibrant patterns or to match your decor.
- Keep the work area clean and organized to avoid tangling of cords, which can affect the hanging's symmetry and neatness.

Expected Result: The finished mini wall hanging should display an attractive pattern of knots and textures, hanging gracefully and evenly from the wooden dowel. The edges should be crisp, and the fringe should be evenly cut, providing a polished look. This project not only serves as a lovely addition to any small space but also as a confidence builder for beginners in Macramé, offering a foundation for more complex projects in the future.

Glass Jar Covers

Project Goal: The goal is to create simple Macramé covers for glass jars, turning them into stylish vases, candle holders, or small storage containers. This project is perfect for beginners to practice basic knotting skills while making useful and attractive home decor items.

Materials Needed:

- Cotton cord, 2mm thickness, about 80 inches per jar
- Scissors
- Measuring tape
- Glass jars of various sizes
- Optional: beads for decoration

Knot Techniques Used:

- Gathering Knot
- Square Knot

Procedure:

Preparation of Materials:
1. Measure and cut the cotton cord into lengths of 80 inches. You will need 6 cords per jar.
2. If using beads, ensure they fit onto the cord and stay in place once secured.

Beginning the Work:
1. Fold each cord in half to create a loop at the midpoint. Use this loop to start the cover with a gathering knot.
2. Secure the loop temporarily to the top of the jar using a simple knot, or attach it to a clipboard to keep it steady.

Project Development:
1. Arrange the cords evenly around the jar.
2. Tie a gathering knot right under the jar's lip to secure all cords.
3. Use four cords to tie a square knot. Continue tying square knots about an inch apart around the jar.
4. For the next row, tie alternating square knots by using two cords from one knot and two from an adjacent knot. This will create a net-like pattern.
5. Keep tying knots until you've covered the desired length of the jar. For shorter jars, cover up to halfway; for taller jars, cover up to three-quarters.
6. Optional: Add beads by threading them onto the cords before knotting to add a decorative touch.

Assembly and Finishing:
1. Finish the cover with another gathering knot at the end of the last row to secure everything.
2. Trim any excess cord beyond the final knot, leaving a small fringe if desired.
3. If using the jar as a candle holder, ensure the upper edge of the cover is below the rim for safety.

Helpful Hints:
- Maintain consistent tension while knotting to ensure a snug fit around the jar.
- Adjust the tightness of the gathering knots based on the jar's use; looser for decoration, tighter for functional use.
- Experiment with different cord colors and thicknesses to match your decor or create themed covers.

Expected Result: The finished glass jar covers should look neat with even knots and a snug fit around the jars. The Macramé should enhance the jar's appearance while adding a handmade touch. Whether used as vases, candle holders, or small storage containers, these covered jars should be both practical and decorative. Added beads can provide a unique and appealing look.

Cell Phone Pouches

Project Goal: The goal is to create a stylish and protective cell phone pouch using basic Macramé techniques. This project is perfect for beginners who want to craft a functional item that safeguards their phone while adding a personalized touch of style.

Materials Needed:
- Cotton or hemp cord, 3mm thickness, approximately 100 inches per pouch
- Scissors
- Measuring tape
- Optional: beads, buttons, or magnetic clasps for closure
- Optional: a small ring or swivel hook for attaching to bags or belts

Knot Techniques Used:
- Lark's Head Knot
- Square Knot
- Vertical Half Hitch

Procedure: Preparation of Materials:
1. Cut the cord into four lengths of 25 inches each.
2. Fold each cord in half to form a loop at the midpoint.

Beginning the Work:
1. Use a Lark's Head Knot to attach each cord to a small horizontal dowel or a sturdy piece of cardboard. This setup will help keep the cords organized and provide tension while you work.

Project Development:
1. Begin by tying a row of Square Knots using the groups of four cords. Arrange the knots tightly together to form the solid back panel of the pouch.
2. Continue with several rows of Square Knots until the panel reaches half the length of the intended phone size. This will form one side of the pouch.
3. To create the sides of the pouch, utilize Vertical Half Hitches along the edges, looping around the outer cords and working vertically. This technique will add structure and define the edges of the pouch.
4. Repeat the process for the other half of the pouch, ensuring that when folded, it will snugly fit the dimensions of a typical cell phone.
5. To join the sides, continue using Vertical Half Hitches to connect the edges at the bottom and sides, leaving the top open.

Assembly and Finishing:
1. Finish the top of the pouch with a decorative row of Square Knots or add a flap that can be secured with a bead, button, or magnetic clasp.

2. Trim any excess cords and optionally fray the ends for a stylish tassel effect.

3. If a carrying loop or attachment is desired, secure a small ring or swivel hook to the upper side of the pouch, ensuring it's firmly knotted and can support the weight of the phone.

Helpful Hints:

- Measure your phone before starting the project to ensure the pouch will have the correct dimensions.
- Choose durable and soft cords to prevent scratching the phone screen.
- If using a closure, ensure it is secure enough to keep the phone from slipping out during daily activities.

Expected Result: The finished cell phone pouch should be snug, providing a soft yet sturdy protective layer around the phone. The Macramé design should be tight enough to hold the phone securely but flexible enough to allow easy access. Decorative elements like beads or a tassel can add personal flair to the pouch, making it not only a practical piece but also a fashionable accessory.

Sunglasses Straps

Project Goal:

The goal of this project is to create functional and stylish sunglasses straps using basic Macramé techniques. These straps are perfect for beginners looking to craft a practical accessory that keeps sunglasses secure while adding a personalized touch of artisanal style.

Materials Needed:

- Cotton or nylon cord, 2mm thickness, approximately 40 inches per strap
- Scissors
- Measuring tape
- Two rubber grips for sunglasses attachment
- Optional: beads or small charms for decoration

Knot Techniques Used:

- Square Knot
- Spiral Knot

Procedure:

Preparation of Materials:

1. Cut the cord into a length of 40 inches.

2. If using beads or charms, prepare these by ensuring they are the right size to slide onto the cord but remain securely in place once positioned.

Beginning the Work:

1. Fold the cord in half to create a midpoint, which will serve as the center of the back neck section of the strap.

Project Development:

1. Start by sliding the two ends of the cord through the holes in each rubber grip attachment, one on each end, ensuring they are positioned at the very ends of the cord.
2. Secure each end with a tight overhand knot to keep the rubber grips from sliding off.
3. Moving towards the center from both ends, begin tying Spiral Knots to create a twisted pattern that adds elasticity and visual interest to the strap. Work about 6 inches of Spiral Knots from both ends towards the center.
4. Meet in the middle with a few Square Knots to provide a stable, non-twisted section that will rest comfortably at the back of the neck.
5. Optionally, incorporate beads or charms along the strap by threading them onto the cords between knots for added decoration.

Assembly and Finishing:

1. Ensure all knots are tight and the ends are securely fastened to prevent the strap from coming loose.
2. Trim any excess cord beyond the finishing knots neatly to keep the ends tidy.
3. Optionally, apply a small amount of clear nail polish or glue to the knots at the ends to further secure the rubber grips and prevent fraying.

Helpful Hints:

- Keep the tension consistent when tying Spiral Knots to ensure the strap has an even, professional look.
- Choose lightweight materials for the beads or charms to prevent the sunglasses strap from becoming too heavy or pulling on the ears.
- Adjust the length of the strap according to personal preference or comfort, making sure it's long enough to hang the sunglasses around the neck when not in use.

Expected Result: The finished sunglasses strap should be lightweight yet durable, holding sunglasses securely around the neck. The Spiral Knots should provide a flexible and attractive look, while the Square Knot section at the back ensures comfort and stability. If beads or charms are added, they should complement the strap's design without overwhelming it. This custom Macramé sunglasses strap is not only practical but also a stylish accessory, perfect for sunny days and outdoor activities.

Home Décor Projects

Basic Plant Hangers

Project Goal:

The goal is to create a basic Macramé plant hanger that serves as a functional and decorative way to display houseplants. This project is ideal for beginners eager to explore the craft of Macramé and to add a touch of greenery to their living space.

Materials Needed:

- Cotton or hemp cord, 4mm thickness, about 100 feet per hanger
- A metal or wooden ring, 2 inches in diameter
- Scissors
- Measuring tape
- Pot to fit the hanger, approximately 6-8 inches in diameter
- Optional: beads or rings for decorative embellishment

Knot Techniques Used:

- Lark's Head Knot
- Square Knot
- Spiral Knot
- Gathering Knot

Procedure:

Preparation of Materials:

1. Cut four lengths of cord, each measuring 25 feet. This length allows for ample room for knotting and adjustments.
2. Fold each length of cord in half to form a loop at the midpoint.

Beginning the Work:

1. Attach the cords to the metal or wooden ring at their midpoints using Lark's Head Knots. This will create eight hanging cords.
2. Hang the ring from a hook or a temporary hanger to facilitate easier knotting.

Project Development:

1. Start about 6 inches down from the ring. Use four cords to tie a Square Knot. Repeat this with the remaining cords so you have a total of four square knots at the same level.

2. Move down another 4 inches and start a series of alternating Square Knots. Take two cords from one group and two from an adjacent group, and tie a Square Knot. Repeat this around to form a net-like structure.

3. Continue this pattern, adding more levels of alternating Square Knots every few inches, according to the height of the pot you intend to use.

4. About halfway to the desired final length, incorporate Spiral Knots for a decorative twist if desired.

5. Test the fit by placing the pot in the hanger to ensure that the knots securely support the pot. Adjust the distance between knot levels if necessary.

Assembly and Finishing:

1. Once the pot fits securely, finish the hanger just below the pot's bottom by gathering all the cords and tying a large Gathering Knot. Ensure this knot is tight and secure.

2. Trim the remaining cord below this knot to your desired length. Optionally, fray or comb out these ends to create a tassel effect.

3. If using beads or decorative rings, thread these onto selected strands either before knotting or incorporate them into the final fringe.

Helpful Hints:

- Ensure all knots are tied tightly and uniformly to prevent the pot from slipping or tilting.
- Adjust the length of the starting cords depending on the final desired length of the hanger and the size of the pot.
- Consider the weight of the pot when selecting cord thickness and knot types to ensure durability and stability.

Expected Result: The finished basic plant hanger should securely hold the pot at the desired height and provide a stable, aesthetically pleasing display for your plant. The knots should be evenly spaced and tightly secured to handle the weight of the plant and pot. This Macramé plant hanger not only serves a practical purpose but also enhances the decor, bringing a natural and handcrafted element into your home.

Simple Wall Hangings

Project Goal:

The goal of this project is to create simple yet elegant Macramé wall hangings that can serve as subtle artistic statements in any living space. This project is perfect for beginners looking to add a touch of handcrafted texture and warmth to their décor.

Materials Needed:

- Cotton or hemp cord, 3mm thickness, about 120 feet per hanging
- Wooden dowel or branch, 12 to 18 inches in length
- Scissors
- Measuring tape
- Optional: beads, wooden rings, or other embellishments

Knot Techniques Used:

- Lark's Head Knot
- Square Knot
- Diagonal Half Hitch

Procedure:

Preparation of Materials:

1. Cut eight lengths of cord, each measuring 15 feet. This length allows for multiple knotting layers and fringe.
2. If you plan to incorporate embellishments like beads or rings, prepare these items by ensuring they fit the cord thickness.

Beginning the Work:

1. Attach each cord to the wooden dowel using Lark's Head Knots, folding each cord in half to create the loop that goes over the dowel. This should result in 16 hanging strands.
2. Secure the dowel horizontally to a working space using hooks or a temporary hanging setup to facilitate easier knotting.

Project Development:

1. Begin with a row of Square Knots using groups of four cords across the entire length of the dowel. This establishes a solid base for the design.
2. Below the initial row, start incorporating Diagonal Half Hitch patterns to create a textured, geometric design. Use one of the outer cords as a lead cord to guide the direction of the knotting.
3. Alternate the direction of the diagonal patterns to create a chevron or diamond shape, depending on your design preference.
4. Continue layering Square Knots and Diagonal Half Hitches to build out the desired pattern and fullness.
5. Periodically step back to assess the hanging's symmetry and adjust as necessary.

Assembly and Finishing:

1. Once the desired length and pattern complexity are achieved, complete the wall hanging by ensuring all knots are secure.

2. Cut the remaining lengths of the cords to create a fringe at the bottom. You can keep the fringe straight or cut it into a shape (e.g., a V or a curve).

3. Optionally, comb out the fringe to create a softer, fuller appearance.

4. Add any planned embellishments, such as threading beads onto some of the fringe strands or attaching rings along parts of the hanging.

Helpful Hints:

- Maintain even tension in your knots for a uniform and neat appearance.

- If using beads or other embellishments, consider their weight and placement to ensure they do not distort the hanging.

- Regularly check the overall balance and symmetry of your piece, especially if it's intended as a focal point in room décor.

Expected Result: The finished wall hanging should display a clean and balanced arrangement of Macramé knots, with a harmonious blend of textures and geometric patterns. The fringe should complement the overall design, providing an elegant finish to the hanging. This piece should serve not only as a beautiful addition to your home decor but also as a testament to the timeless appeal of handcrafted textile art.

Coasters and Table Mats

Project Goal:

The goal of this project is to create functional and decorative coasters and table mats that protect surfaces while adding a stylish touch to the dining or coffee table. This beginner-friendly project is perfect for learning basic Macramé techniques and producing practical items for home use or as gifts.

Materials Needed:

- Cotton or hemp cord, 4mm thickness, about 50 feet per coaster or mat
- Scissors
- Measuring tape
- Optional: wooden or ceramic beads for decorative accents

Knot Techniques Used:

- Square Knot
- Spiral Knot
- Gathering Knot

Procedure:

Preparation of Materials:

1. For coasters, cut the cord into lengths of about 10 feet each. For larger table mats, cut lengths of about 20 feet each.

2. If using beads for decoration, prepare them by ensuring the holes are large enough to fit the cord but snug enough to stay in place.

Beginning the Work:

1. Fold each cord in half to form a loop at the midpoint, which will be the center of the coaster or mat.

Project Development:

1. Begin by securing the loop under a clipboard or pinning it to a corkboard to keep it stable.

2. Start with a series of Square Knots, radiating outward from the central loop. Use four strands for each knot, alternating the center strands and the knotting strands to create a dense and even texture.

3. Introduce Spiral Knots for a decorative twisted pattern, especially effective around the edges of the coaster or mat.

4. Continue expanding the work by adding more Square Knots and Spiral Knots until you reach the desired diameter—typically about 4 inches for coasters and 12-15 inches for table mats.

5. If incorporating beads, thread them onto the cords where desired, securing them into place with a knot below each bead.

Assembly and Finishing:

1. To finish the coaster or mat, tie a Gathering Knot at the outer edge to neatly gather and secure all the cords.

2. Trim the excess cords to create a clean, uniform edge, or leave a fringe if preferred.

3. If a fringe is chosen, comb out the ends to ensure a soft, even look.

Helpful Hints:

- Maintain consistent tension throughout the project to ensure the coaster or mat lies flat and even.

- Adjust the size of the loops at the beginning and the tightness of your knots to control the final size of the coaster or mat.

- Consider waterproofing your finished products if they will be used with wet dishes or glasses to protect the material and maintain their appearance.

Expected Result: The finished coasters and table mats should be sturdy and lay flat against surfaces, with a consistent pattern and neat edges. They should serve not only as a protective layer but also as a decorative element for your table setting. The optional beads can add a touch of elegance, making these items lovely additions to your home décor or thoughtful handmade gifts.

Decorative Bottle Covers

Project Goal:

The objective of this project is to create decorative Macramé bottle covers that serve as stylish accents to ordinary glass bottles, transforming them into striking décor pieces or thoughtful gifts. This project is perfect for beginners who want to enhance their knotting skills while crafting unique and eye-catching home accessories.

Materials Needed:

- Cotton or hemp cord, 2mm thickness, about 60 feet per bottle cover
- Scissors
- Measuring tape
- Glass bottles of various shapes and sizes
- Optional: beads or small rings to embellish the covers

Knot Techniques Used:

- Lark's Head Knot
- Square Knot
- Spiral Knot
- Gathering Knot

Procedure:

Preparation of Materials:

1. Cut the cord into lengths of about 15 feet each. Depending on the size of the bottle, you may need 4 to 6 lengths per cover.
2. If using beads or rings, ensure they can be threaded onto the cord and will stay securely in place.

Beginning the Work:

1. Fold each length of cord in half to find the center and create a loop.
2. Attach each cord to the neck of the bottle using a Lark's Head Knot, distributing them evenly around the bottle's neck.

Project Development:

1. Begin by tying a base row of Square Knots around the neck of the bottle, using four cords for each knot.
2. Continue with additional rows of Square Knots, gradually working down the shape of the bottle. Adjust the spacing and tightness of the knots based on the contour of the bottle to ensure a snug fit.
3. Introduce Spiral Knots to add a decorative twist as you move down the bottle. This technique can be used to create distinct textured patterns that enhance the aesthetic appeal of the cover.
4. Optionally, incorporate beads or rings by threading them onto the cords before continuing with the knots to add visual interest and personalized flair.
5. Continue knotting until you have covered the desired area of the bottle. For a full cover, continue to the base; for a partial cover, you might stop at the midsection or wherever suits your design.

Assembly and Finishing:

1. To secure the cover, finish with a Wrapping Knot at the last row of your design or at the base of the bottle, ensuring all cords are tightly gathered and the cover will not slip off.
2. Trim any excess cord and tuck in the ends to maintain a clean, polished look.

3. Optionally, if a fringe is desired at the bottom or top edge, leave extra cord length and comb it out to create a soft fringe effect.

Helpful Hints:

- Ensure that each knot is tied consistently to maintain an even and symmetrical appearance on the bottle.
- Choose the thickness and color of the cord based on the style and usage of the bottle, considering how the texture and color will complement its contents or surroundings.
- If the bottle will be used for liquids, consider using synthetic cords for better moisture resistance.

Expected Result: The finished Macramé bottle covers should fit snugly around each bottle, enhancing its silhouette with beautifully patterned knots and textures. The embellishments should add a personalized touch without overwhelming the simplicity of the design. These covers not only elevate the aesthetic value of ordinary bottles but also serve as creative and eco-friendly ways to repurpose and display them in your home or give them as handmade gifts.

Elegant Fruit Bowls

Project Goal:

The goal of this project is to create elegant Macramé fruit bowls that serve both functional and decorative purposes in a home setting. This beginner-friendly project allows crafters to produce a unique vessel for holding fruits or other items while enhancing their space with a handcrafted touch.

Materials Needed:

- Cotton or hemp cord, 5mm thickness, about 120 feet per bowl
- A large bowl or a balloon to use as a mold
- Scissors
- Measuring tape
- Optional: waterproofing spray to protect the finished bowl

Knot Techniques Used:

- Wrapped Knot
- Square Knot
- Half Hitch

Procedure:

Preparation of Materials:

1. Cut the cord into lengths of about 30 feet each. You will need 4 lengths for this project.
2. If using a bowl as a mold, choose one that has the desired shape and size for your finished fruit bowl.

Beginning the Work:

1. Use the bowl or inflated balloon as a mold by placing it upside down on your working surface.
2. Begin by wrapping one length of cord around the mold to determine the base size and mark where the cord meets. Tie a Wrapped Knot at this point to create the starting base of the bowl.

Project Development:

1. Arrange the cords around the circumference of the mold, using Lark's Head Knots to secure them evenly spaced apart.
2. Begin tying Square Knots using the cords, ensuring each knot is tight and evenly spaced to form the sides of the bowl. Use groups of four cords for each knot.
3. Continue adding rows of Square Knots, working upwards and ensuring each row is snug against the previous to create a sturdy structure.
4. As the bowl begins to take shape, you can introduce Half Hitch knots for added texture and decorative detail.
5. Continue working until you have reached the desired height of the bowl. Ensure that the knots are close enough to hold items but also provide aesthetic appeal.

Assembly and Finishing:

1. Once the desired height is achieved, finish the top edge with a row of Wrapped Knots for a clean and polished look.
2. Carefully remove the bowl or balloon from inside the Macramé structure.
3. Trim any excess cords and tuck in the ends underneath nearby knots to secure them out of sight.
4. Optional: Apply a layer of waterproofing spray to make the bowl more durable and suitable for holding real fruit or other items that might emit moisture.

Helpful Hints:

- Make sure the mold is stable and won't roll or shift as you work, as this can lead to an uneven shape.

- Adjust the tightness of your knots based on the flexibility you desire in the finished bowl. Tighter knots will create a stiffer bowl.
- Consider the end use of the bowl when choosing materials; for example, synthetic cords may be better for outdoor use.

Expected Result: The finished Macramé fruit bowl should be sturdy and hold its shape well, with a beautifully textured exterior made up of intricate knots. The top edge should be smooth and even, providing a polished appearance. This elegant bowl is not only a practical item for storing fruits but also a striking piece of decor that reflects the craftsmanship and creativity of its maker.

Chic Napkin Rings

Project Goal:

The objective of this project is to create chic Macramé napkin rings that add a sophisticated and personalized touch to table settings. This beginner-friendly project allows crafters to design functional yet decorative elements perfect for enhancing the dining experience during special occasions or everyday meals.

Materials Needed:

- Cotton or hemp cord, 2mm thickness, about 10 feet per napkin ring
- Scissors
- Measuring tape
- Optional: small beads or charms for embellishment

Knot Techniques Used:

- Square Knot
- Gathering Knot

Procedure:

Preparation of Materials:

1. Cut the cord into lengths of about 2.5 feet each. This measurement allows for ample cord to work with for knotting and adjustments.
2. If using beads or charms, ensure they are prepared by checking that they fit the cord and are ready to be threaded as needed.

Beginning the Work:

1. Begin by looping one end of the cord around to form a small ring, roughly the diameter of a typical napkin ring (about 1.5 to 2 inches across).

Project Development:

1. Secure the base loop with a Gathering Knot to keep the initial shape firm and ready for further knotting.

2. Start wrapping the long end of the cord around the loop, covering the initial gathering knot as you go to create a neat and cohesive look.

3. Introduce Square Knots after a few wraps to add texture and pattern to the ring. Continue alternating between simple wraps and square knots around the entire loop.

4. If incorporating beads or charms, thread them onto the cord before making a knot to secure them in place. This can be done intermittently to add a decorative accent.

5. Continue this pattern until the entire ring is covered, ensuring that each wrap and knot is tight and evenly spaced.

Assembly and Finishing:

1. Once the desired pattern and coverage are achieved, finish the end with another Gathering Knot to secure all loose ends and ensure the ring holds its shape.

2. Trim any excess cord close to the end knot, and if necessary, dab a small amount of glue on the knots to prevent fraying.

3. Optionally, smooth out any irregularities in the wrapping or adjust the beads to ensure they are featured prominently and evenly spaced.

Helpful Hints:

- Keep the tension consistent while wrapping and knotting to ensure the napkin ring maintains its circular shape and structural integrity.

- Choose colors and materials that complement your dining decor or thematic elements of your dinnerware.

- Test the ring with a napkin before completing to ensure it fits comfortably and slides easily without being too loose.

Expected Result: The finished Macramé napkin rings should be uniform in size and shape, featuring a sophisticated blend of knotted textures and optional decorative elements like beads. Each ring should snugly fit around a napkin, enhancing its presentation with a handcrafted, elegant appearance. These napkin rings not only serve as practical dining accessories but also as conversation pieces that reflect attention to detail and a flair for creativity in table setting.

Mirror Frames

Project Goal:

The goal of this project is to create decorative Macramé mirror frames that enhance the aesthetic appeal of standard mirrors, transforming them into striking pieces of wall art. This project is perfect for beginners who want to explore larger scale Macramé projects and add a unique, handcrafted touch to their home décor.

Materials Needed:

- Cotton or hemp cord, 5mm thickness, about 200 feet per frame
- Circular or square mirror base
- Scissors
- Measuring tape
- Optional: beads, feathers, or other decorative items for embellishment

Knot Techniques Used:

- Lark's Head Knot
- Square Knot
- Diagonal Half Hitch

Procedure:

Preparation of Materials:

1. Cut the cord into lengths of about 50 feet each. You will need four lengths for this project.
2. Prepare any decorative items such as beads or feathers by ensuring they can be integrated into the Macramé knots or attached securely to the finished frame.

Beginning the Work:

1. Attach each cord to the perimeter of the mirror base using Lark's Head Knots, spacing them evenly around the edge. Ensure the mirror is securely mounted or placed on a flat surface to facilitate easier knotting.

Project Development:

1. Start with a row of Square Knots around the entire edge of the mirror to create a solid foundation for the frame.
2. Continue with additional rows of Square Knots, building out from the edge to create the desired width of the frame. Use groups of four cords for each knot to ensure uniformity and strength.

3. Introduce Diagonal Half Hitches to add texture and decorative patterns within the frame. This technique can be used to create geometric designs or to frame specific sections of the mirror for visual interest.

4. As the frame develops, periodically step back to assess the symmetry and aesthetic balance. Adjust your knotting technique or add more rows as necessary to achieve the desired look.

5. If incorporating beads or other embellishments, thread them onto the cords at desired intervals, securing them with knots to ensure they stay in place.

Assembly and Finishing:

1. Once the desired size and decoration of the frame are achieved, finish off by securing the ends with a final row of Square Knots, ensuring all cords are tightly fastened.

2. Trim any excess cord and neatly tuck in the ends to maintain a clean, polished appearance around the entire frame.

3. Optionally, attach feathers, beads, or other decorative items to the outer edge of the frame or at key focal points to enhance the artistic flair of the piece.

Helpful Hints:

- Maintain even tension in your knots to ensure the frame is sturdy and hangs evenly.
- Consider the overall weight of the finished frame; ensure it's not too heavy for the wall mounting or for the structure of the mirror.
- Choose cord colors that complement or contrast with the wall color where the mirror will be hung to maximize its decorative impact.

Expected Result: The finished Macramé mirror frame should beautifully encase the mirror, adding texture and artistic detail that transforms the mirror into a focal point of any room. The knots should be uniform and tightly secured, with embellishments adding a personalized touch to the design. This project not only serves as a functional mirror but also as an impressive piece of Macramé art that enhances the interior décor with its craftsmanship and style.

Entryway Key and Mail Organizers

Project Goal:

The objective of this project is to create a functional and stylish Macramé key and mail organizer for entryways. This beginner-friendly project is perfect for those looking to enhance their home organization with a handcrafted, decorative touch that is both practical and visually appealing.

Materials Needed:

- Cotton or hemp cord, 4mm thickness, about 150 feet

- Wooden dowel or small curtain rod, about 12 to 18 inches in length
- Small hooks or clips for keys
- Scissors
- Measuring tape
- Optional: wooden or metal rings for decoration

Knot Techniques Used:

- Lark's Head Knot
- Square Knot
- Clove Hitch

Procedure:

Preparation of Materials:

1. Cut the cord into lengths of about 30 feet each. You will need five lengths for this project.
2. Prepare the wooden dowel by ensuring it's smooth and free of any splinters. If using, attach small hooks or clips evenly spaced along the dowel.

Beginning the Work:

1. Attach each cord to the wooden dowel using Lark's Head Knots, spacing them evenly across the dowel. This setup forms the foundation of the organizer.

Project Development:

1. Begin with a row of Square Knots using groups of four cords just below the dowel. This row serves as the structural base for the organizer.
2. Continue adding additional rows of Square Knots, creating a tight mesh that will form the back panel of the organizer, suitable for holding mail or small items securely.
3. Introduce sections separated by Clove Hitch rows to create distinct areas within the organizer for different types of mail or items.
4. To create pouches or pockets, use Clove Hitches to gather sections of the panel at various intervals, creating bulges that can expand slightly to hold items.
5. Throughout the development, periodically check the tension and adjust the spacing to ensure the organizer is functional and aesthetically pleasing.

Assembly and Finishing:

1. Finish the bottom of the organizer with a final row of Square Knots to ensure everything is secure and that the organizer maintains its shape.
2. Trim any excess cord at the bottom and fray the ends for a decorative tassel effect, enhancing the handcrafted look.

3. If using, add wooden or metal rings by attaching them to the sides or bottom of the organizer for additional decorative flair or to hang further items like umbrellas or scarves.

Helpful Hints:

- Ensure the knots are tight and evenly spaced to support the weight of keys, mail, and other items without sagging.
- Consider the items you plan to store when designing the size and number of pouches or compartments.
- Use high-quality, durable materials to withstand daily use and the weight of stored items.

Expected Result: The finished Macramé key and mail organizer should be sturdy and functional, with a distinctively crafted look that enhances the entryway. The knots should be secure, and the overall design should offer practical storage solutions while being a decorative piece. This organizer not only keeps essential items neatly arranged but also adds a touch of artisanal charm to home organization.

Functional Items

Macramé Tote Bags

Project Goal:

The objective of this project is to create a functional and stylish Macramé tote bag that is perfect for everyday use. This project will allow beginners to develop their skills while producing a practical item that showcases the versatility and beauty of Macramé.

Materials Needed:

- Cotton or hemp cord, 5mm thickness, about 300 feet
- Two wooden or metal rings for handles, each 5 inches in diameter
- Scissors
- Measuring tape

Knot Techniques Used:

- Lark's Head Knot
- Square Knot
- Diagonal Half Hitch

Procedure:

Preparation of Materials:

1. Cut the cord into lengths of about 30 feet each. You will need approximately 10 lengths for a medium-sized tote bag.
2. Ensure the wooden or metal rings are smooth and free of any sharp edges to prevent damage to the cords or discomfort during use.

Beginning the Work:

1. Attach each cord to one of the wooden or metal rings using Lark's Head Knots, ensuring they are evenly spaced. This ring will act as the top of one side of the tote bag.

Project Development:

1. Start by tying a row of Square Knots around the ring using groups of four cords. This will form the structural base of the bag.
2. Continue with additional rows of Square Knots to create the body of the bag. As you work your way down, keep the knots tight and evenly spaced.
3. Gradually expand the width of the bag by increasing the space between knots if a wider bottom is desired, or maintain a rectangular shape by keeping the knotting uniform.

4. Introduce Diagonal Half Hitches to add texture and visual interest. This technique can also be used to incorporate a decorative pattern or logo into the design.

5. Once the front side of the bag reaches the desired length, repeat the process for the back side of the bag, starting from the second wooden or metal ring.

Assembly and Finishing:

1. Join the front and back sides of the bag at the sides and bottom using Square Knots to ensure the bag is secure and capable of holding weight.

2. Check the integrity of the bag by applying slight pressure to ensure knots are secure and the bag can hold everyday items.

3. Trim any excess cords at the bottom and inside seams, ensuring they are tucked and hidden for a neat finish.

4. Optional: Add a lining inside the bag by sewing a fabric that complements the Macramé for added durability and to prevent small items from slipping through the knots.

Helpful Hints:

- Consistency is key in ensuring that the bag is symmetrical and balanced.
- Consider using a color or combination of colors that will match well with everyday wear.
- Treat the bag with a fabric or waterproof spray to enhance durability and resistance to wear and stains.

Expected Result: The finished Macramé tote bag should be sturdy, functional, and fashionable, with a neatly crafted pattern and strong handles for easy carrying. It should be spacious enough to carry daily essentials such as books, a small laptop, or groceries, providing not only a practical carryall solution but also a statement piece that reflects the craftsmanship and creativity of Macramé.

Stylish Belts and Accessories

Project Goal:

The aim of this project is to create stylish Macramé belts and accessories that complement everyday attire or enhance special outfits. This project enables beginners to practice precise knotting techniques while crafting fashionable items that showcase their creativity and skill in Macramé.

Materials Needed:

- Cotton or hemp cord, 3mm thickness, about 50 feet for a belt
- Scissors

- Measuring tape
- Belt buckle or loop and end cap for finishing
- Optional: beads or decorative items for embellishment

Knot Techniques Used:

- Square Knot
- Josephine Knot (a variation of the lover's knot for decorative appeal)
- Half Hitch

Procedure:

Preparation of Materials:

1. Cut the cord into lengths of about 10 feet each, depending on the desired length and thickness of the belt.
2. Prepare any additional decorative items such as beads or metal accents to integrate into the design.

Beginning the Work:

1. If using a belt buckle, start by securing one end of the cord to the buckle with a secure knot or by looping it through the buckle and using a Lark's Head Knot.

Project Development:

1. Begin the belt by tying a series of Square Knots to create a strong and flexible foundation.
2. Introduce Josephine Knots at intervals for a distinctive decorative pattern that adds character and style to the belt. This knot creates a striking symmetrical design ideal for focal points along the belt.
3. Continue with Square Knots, alternating with sections of Josephine Knots as desired to enhance the belt's design.
4. If embellishments are part of your design, thread beads onto the cords where they will complement the knots, securing them in place with small knots or by incorporating them into the knotting pattern.
5. Use Half Hitches along the length for added texture and detail, which also helps to strengthen the belt.

Assembly and Finishing:

1. Once the desired length is reached, finish the end of the belt by securing it to the second part of the buckle or adding an end cap if no buckle is used.
2. Ensure all knots are tightly secured and trim any excess cord.
3. Optional: apply a fabric protector to enhance the belt's durability and stain resistance.

Helpful Hints:

- Ensure that all knots are evenly spaced and consistently tight to maintain the belt's shape and function.
- Choose cord colors that match or contrast well with your wardrobe, considering the outfits with which the belt will be worn.
- Regularly measure the belt against your waist or hips to ensure a perfect fit as you progress through the knotting.

Expected Result: The finished Macramé belt should be sturdy, stylish, and functional, with a clean and professional appearance. The Josephine Knots should provide elegant detailing, making the belt not just a utility item but a statement accessory. Any added beads or decorative elements should enhance the belt's aesthetic without overwhelming the intricate knotting. This custom Macramé belt will not only serve as a practical wardrobe piece but also as a testament to the wearer's taste for uniquely handcrafted accessories.

Grocery Bag Holders

Project Goal:

The aim of this project is to create a functional Macramé grocery bag holder that is both stylish and practical for organizing and storing plastic bags in a kitchen or utility room. This beginner-friendly project allows crafters to make a useful item that helps reduce clutter and adds a handmade touch to home organization.

Materials Needed:

- Cotton or hemp cord, 3mm thickness, about 100 feet
- Scissors
- Measuring tape
- A small ring or loop for hanging
- Optional: elastic band for the top or bottom openings

Knot Techniques Used:

- Lark's Head Knot
- Square Knot
- Alternating Square Knot

Procedure:

Preparation of Materials:

1. Cut the cord into lengths of about 10 feet each. You will need about 10 lengths for a standard-sized grocery bag holder.
2. Prepare the ring or loop for hanging by ensuring it's sturdy enough to support the weight of the bag when filled.

Beginning the Work:

1. Attach each cord to the ring using Lark's Head Knots, spreading them evenly around the ring. This setup forms the top hanging point of the bag holder.

Project Development:

1. Begin by tying a foundational row of Square Knots using the hanging cords, approximately 2 inches down from the ring. This creates a stable and decorative top edge.
2. Continue adding additional rows of Square Knots, about 1 inch apart, to start forming the sides of the bag holder. Use groups of four cords for each knot.
3. Introduce Alternating Square Knots after a few rows to begin expanding the body of the bag holder. This technique helps create a mesh-like structure that is both stretchable and strong, ideal for storing multiple bags.
4. As you work downwards, adjust the knot tightness and spacing based on the desired width and elasticity of the holder. If using an elastic band, incorporate it into the design by threading it through a row of knots at the opening to provide a retractable closure.
5. Continue knotting until the holder reaches the desired length, typically about 18 to 24 inches long.

Assembly and Finishing:

1. To finish the bottom of the bag holder, gradually reduce the spacing between knots to taper the holder, securing all cords with a final gathering knot.
2. Trim any excess cords and tuck in the ends neatly for a polished look.
3. Optional: If not using an elastic band, create a tight closure at the bottom using several tight rows of knots to prevent bags from slipping out.

Helpful Hints:

- Ensure that knots are evenly spaced and consistent for both aesthetic appeal and functional strength.
- Consider using a color or pattern of cord that matches your kitchen or utility room décor.

- Regularly test the stretch and capacity of the bag holder as you knot, ensuring it meets your storage needs.

Expected Result: The finished Macramé grocery bag holder should be a stylish and practical addition to your home, offering an organized solution for storing grocery bags. The mesh-like knotting should provide flexibility to accommodate multiple bags while retaining its shape. The holder should hang securely and provide easy access to bags when needed, blending functionality with the unique charm of handmade Macramé.

Yoga Mat Straps

Project Goal:

The goal of this project is to create functional and stylish yoga mat straps that allow for easy transport of a yoga mat while incorporating the artistic flair of Macramé. This project is perfect for beginners who want to combine functionality with handcrafted design in their daily activities.

Materials Needed:

- Cotton or hemp cord, 4mm thickness, about 50 feet
- Two metal or wooden rings, each about 2 inches in diameter
- Scissors
- Measuring tape

Knot Techniques Used:

- Square Knot
- Spiral Knot

Procedure:

Preparation of Materials:

1. Cut the cord into two lengths of 25 feet each.
2. If using, prepare the metal or wooden rings by ensuring they are smooth and free of any sharp edges.

Beginning the Work:

1. Fold each length of cord in half to find the midpoint and create a loop.

Project Development:

1. Begin by attaching each loop through a ring using a Lark's Head Knot. This will secure the cord to the ring and serve as the starting point for each strap.
2. Start tying Square Knots right below the ring, using the four strands that come out from the Lark's Head Knot. Continue with about a foot of Square Knots for a strong, supportive start.

3. Transition into Spiral Knots to create a twisted design for the strap. Continue this pattern until you reach about halfway down the length of the strap.

4. Return to Square Knots for the remaining length to ensure stability and durability.

5. Measure the strap around your rolled yoga mat occasionally to gauge the length and adjust accordingly to ensure a snug fit.

Assembly and Finishing:

1. Once you have reached the desired length, thread the ends of the cords through the second ring.

2. Secure the cords with a series of tight Square Knots just below the second ring to prevent slippage.

3. Finish off by trimming any excess cord and optionally sealing the ends with a fray check solution or a light application of clear glue to prevent unraveling.

4. Optional: If additional security is desired, you can add a sliding knot or bead below each ring to adjust the tightness of the strap.

Helpful Hints:

- Keep the tension consistent while knotting to ensure the strap maintains an even and attractive appearance.
- Choose a durable, weather-resistant cord if you plan to use the strap outdoors.
- Consider customizing the color of the cord to match or complement your yoga mat.

Expected Result: The finished yoga mat straps should be both durable and decorative, easily wrapping around a rolled yoga mat to facilitate comfortable carrying. The knots should be tight and evenly spaced, providing a secure hold while adding a touch of Macramé elegance. This practical accessory will not only make transporting your yoga mat easier but also express your personal style and appreciation for handmade crafts.

Camera Straps

Project Goal:

The aim of this project is to create durable and stylish camera straps that not only provide functionality and security for carrying cameras but also exhibit the craft of Macramé. This project allows beginners to enhance their knotting skills while producing a fashionable and useful accessory for photography enthusiasts.

Materials Needed:

- Cotton or hemp cord, 3mm thickness, about 80 feet

- Two metal clips or swivel hooks, suitable for attaching to camera loops
- Scissors
- Measuring tape
- Optional: leather or fabric pads for shoulder comfort

Knot Techniques Used:

- Square Knot
- Josephine Knot (for decorative elements)
- Double Half Hitch

Procedure:

Preparation of Materials:

1. Cut the cord into two lengths of 40 feet each. This allows for plenty of length to work with, considering the doubling over and knotting required.
2. Prepare the metal clips or hooks by ensuring they are sturdy and free from rust or damage.

Beginning the Work:

1. Fold each length of cord in half to find the midpoint. Start by attaching the midpoint of one cord length to one of the metal clips using a secure Lark's Head Knot.

Project Development:

1. Begin with a series of Square Knots, making a broad, flat band. This will form the main part of the strap that goes around the neck and shoulders.
2. After about 20 inches of Square Knots, incorporate Josephine Knots at intervals for a stylish, intricate pattern that enhances the visual appeal of the strap.
3. Continue with more Square Knots, ensuring even tension and consistency for durability and aesthetic uniformity.
4. If a shoulder pad is used, integrate it by wrapping the macramé around the pad, securing it with Double Half Hitches to hold the pad in place securely.
5. As you near the end of the desired length, transition to a series of Double Half Hitches, which will help taper the strap towards the second metal clip.
6. Repeat the knotting sequence for the second half of the strap, ensuring symmetry in design and length.

Assembly and Finishing:

1. Attach the end of each cord to the second metal clip using a combination of Knots and Hitches to ensure security.

2. Trim any excess cord and carefully burn or seal the ends to prevent fraying, using a lighter or fray-check solution.

3. Test the strap by attaching it to a camera and adjusting to check for comfort and balance.

Helpful Hints:

- Regularly check the strap length against your body to ensure it hangs comfortably and provides easy access to your camera.

- Choose cords in colors that complement or contrast nicely with your camera or personal style.

- Ensure all knots are very tight, as the strap needs to support the weight of the camera securely.

Expected Result: The finished camera strap should be strong, functional, and visually appealing, with intricate knots and a professional finish. It should comfortably support the camera's weight and distribute it evenly across the shoulders. The custom Macramé camera strap not only enhances the camera's accessibility and safety but also adds a touch of personalized style to your photography gear.

Laptop Sleeves

Project Goal:

The objective of this project is to create a protective and stylish Macramé laptop sleeve that provides a snug cover for laptops, combining functionality with aesthetic appeal. This beginner-friendly project allows crafters to design a custom piece that not only safeguards electronic devices but also displays intricate knotting work.

Materials Needed:

- Cotton or hemp cord, 4mm thickness, about 200 feet
- Scissors
- Measuring tape
- Button or toggle for closure
- Optional: fabric lining for additional protection

Knot Techniques Used:

- Square Knot
- Diagonal Half Hitch
- Vertical Clove Hitch

Procedure:

Preparation of Materials:

1. Cut the cord into lengths of about 50 feet each. Four strands will be required to create a dense, protective layer.

2. If using, prepare the fabric lining by cutting it to the size of the laptop, adding an extra inch around all sides for seam allowance.

Beginning the Work:

1. Fold each length of cord in half to establish the midpoint, which will serve as the bottom center of the laptop sleeve.

Project Development:

1. Begin by attaching the cords to a horizontal support, like a rod or dowel, using Lark's Head Knots at the midpoint. This setup facilitates symmetrical knotting from the center outwards.

2. Start with a row of Square Knots forming the base of the sleeve. Ensure the knots are tight and evenly spaced.

3. Continue knotting upward, alternating between Square Knots and Diagonal Half Hitches to create a decorative yet dense fabric that offers padding and protection. The Diagonal Half Hitches add a textural element and strength to the sleeve.

4. Use Vertical Clove Hitches along the sides to bind the edges together as you approach the desired height of the laptop.

5. Measure the width periodically to ensure the sleeve will snugly fit the laptop, adjusting knot tightness as necessary.

Assembly and Finishing:

1. Once the sleeve reaches the top of the laptop, finish with a series of Square Knots to close the top edge, leaving an opening for sliding the laptop in and out.

2. Attach a button or toggle near the top opening, and create a loop on the opposite side with remaining cords, ensuring it's secure and easy to fasten.

3. Trim excess cords and optionally seal the ends to prevent fraying.

4. If adding a fabric lining, stitch it inside the Macramé sleeve, securing it along the top edge and sides for a smooth finish that protects the laptop from scratches.

Helpful Hints:

- Consistency in knot tension is crucial for creating a sleeve that fits properly.
- Choose a durable, soft cord to prevent scratching the laptop.

- Regularly check the fit by carefully placing the laptop inside the sleeve as you progress to ensure a custom fit.

Expected Result: The finished Macramé laptop sleeve should be snug, offering a stylish yet protective layer for the laptop. The knots should provide cushioning and the design elements, such as the Diagonal Half Hitches, should add both visual interest and structural integrity. The closure should be secure yet easy to use for quick access. This handcrafted sleeve not only serves as a functional accessory but also demonstrates the versatility and beauty of Macramé craft.

Water Bottle Carriers

Project Goal:

The aim of this project is to create functional and stylish Macramé water bottle carriers that are perfect for on-the-go hydration. This beginner-friendly project allows crafters to create a practical accessory that securely holds a water bottle while adding a touch of handcrafted elegance.

Materials Needed:

- Cotton or hemp cord, 3mm thickness, about 80 feet
- One metal or wooden ring, approximately 2 inches in diameter for the handle
- Scissors
- Measuring tape
- Optional: beads or charms for decoration

Knot Techniques Used:

- Lark's Head Knot
- Square Knot
- Spiral Knot
- Gathering Knot

Procedure:

Preparation of Materials:

1. Cut the cord into lengths of about 20 feet each. You will need four of these for a strong and durable carrier.
2. If using, prepare beads or charms by ensuring they can be easily threaded onto the cord.

Beginning the Work:

1. Fold each length of cord in half to create a loop at the midpoint. Attach each loop to the metal or wooden ring using Lark's Head Knots. This will create the top handle of the carrier.

Project Development:

1. Begin by tying a series of Square Knots below the ring, using groups of four cords. This forms the neck of the carrier and provides stability for the bottle.

2. Continue with a series of alternating Square Knots, expanding the mesh to accommodate the width of the bottle. This method helps create a flexible yet snug fit around the bottle.

3. Incorporate Spiral Knots for added design and to ensure the body of the carrier is aesthetically pleasing as well as functional.

4. As you approach the base of the bottle, reduce the gaps between knots to prepare for the bottom closure.

5. Use a Gathering Knot to neatly gather all the cords at the base, securing them tightly to form a solid bottom that prevents the bottle from slipping out.

Assembly and Finishing:

1. Ensure all knots are tight and the carrier securely conforms to the shape of the bottle.

2. Trim any excess cord at the bottom and melt or glue the tips to prevent fraying.

3. Optional: Thread beads or attach charms at strategic points on the carrier for decoration, ensuring they do not interfere with the functionality.

4. Test the carrier by inserting the water bottle to ensure a secure fit.

Helpful Hints:

- Adjust the length of the cords and the tightness of the knots depending on the size and shape of the water bottle.

- Choose a durable, water-resistant cord material if the carrier will be used outdoors.

- Regularly check the fit of the bottle during the knotting process to ensure the carrier is neither too tight nor too loose.

Expected Result: The finished Macramé water bottle carrier should be sturdy, functional, and stylish, with a solid base and secure sides that comfortably hold the water bottle. The handle should be strong enough to support the weight of a full bottle, and the overall design should reflect the practicality and elegance of Macramé artistry. This carrier not only makes transporting water convenient but also serves as a chic accessory for everyday use.

Earbud Cases

Project Goal:

The goal of this project is to create functional and stylish Macramé earbud cases that protect and store earbuds conveniently. This beginner-friendly project enables crafters to create a small, portable accessory that helps prevent tangles and damage to earbuds, adding a personalized touch of handcrafted style.

Materials Needed:

- Cotton or hemp cord, 2mm thickness, about 30 feet
- A small button or toggle for closure
- Scissors
- Measuring tape

Knot Techniques Used:

- Square Knot
- Spiral Knot
- Buttonhole Knot (for creating a closure)

Procedure:

Preparation of Materials:

1. Cut the cord into lengths of about 5 feet each. You will need six of these lengths to create a durable and dense case.
2. Prepare the button or toggle by ensuring it is small enough to be discrete yet functional for securing the case.

Beginning the Work:

1. Gather all the cords and align them by their centers. Use an initial Square Knot to bind them together, creating the starting point for the case.

Project Development:

1. Begin by creating a flat circle base using Square Knots. Arrange the cords in a circle and tie Square Knots around the perimeter, gradually expanding outward by adding small gaps between the knots to increase the circle's size.
2. Once the base is large enough to cover the bottom of the earbuds (about 2-3 inches in diameter), start building the sides by stacking Square Knots directly above the previous row without expanding, allowing the walls to rise vertically.

3. Introduce Spiral Knots after a few rows of Square Knots to add a decorative twist to the sides of the case. This pattern can be continued up the height of the case or alternated with more Square Knots for textural variation.

4. When nearing the desired height of the case (typically about 2 inches, enough to comfortably fit earbuds), start decreasing the number of cords used in each knot to taper the opening slightly.

5. Finish the top with a row of Buttonhole Knots, creating a loop large enough for the button or toggle to fit through, ensuring it acts as a secure closure.

Assembly and Finishing:

1. Sew or firmly attach the button or toggle opposite the buttonhole loop on the body of the case.

2. Trim any excess cord from the top and carefully melt or apply a small amount of glue to the ends to prevent fraying.

3. Optionally, decorate the case with additional beads or charms by incorporating them into the knots as you work or attaching them at the end for a personalized touch.

Helpful Hints:

- Keep knots tight and uniform to ensure the case is sturdy and holds its shape.
- Regularly test the fit by placing the earbuds inside the case as you progress to ensure a snug and secure fit.
- Choose a closure method that is easy to manipulate, especially when on the go.

Expected Result: The finished Macramé earbud case should be compact, functional, and aesthetically pleasing, with a secure closure that keeps earbuds safely stored. The design should be seamless and tidy, providing easy access while preventing tangles and damage to the earbuds. This small, practical project not only serves as a great way to protect earbuds but also showcases the versatility and beauty of Macramé in everyday items.

Modern Macramé: Innovative Projects for Beginners

Table Runners

Project Goal: The goal of this project is to create a beautiful Macramé table runner that serves as a stunning centerpiece for dining or coffee tables. This project allows beginners to practice their knotting skills while creating an elegant piece for home decor.

Materials Needed:

- Cotton or hemp cord, 3mm thickness, about 300 feet
- Scissors
- Measuring tape
- Optional: beads or decorative items for added embellishment

Knot Techniques Used:

- Square Knot
- Lark's Head Knot

Procedure: Preparation of Materials:

1. Cut the cord into lengths of about 30 feet each. You will need several lengths depending on the desired width and length of the table runner.
2. If using, prepare beads or decorative items by ensuring they can be integrated into the Macramé design.

Beginning the Work:

1. Start by measuring and cutting a length of cord to serve as the core foundation, which will run the entire length of the desired table runner. This core cord should be twice the length of the finished runner plus extra for adjustments.

Project Development:

1. Attach cords to the core foundation using Lark's Head Knots spaced evenly across the width of the runner.
2. Begin creating the body of the runner by tying a continuous row of Square Knots along the attached cords, forming the initial structure.

3. Continue with rows of Square Knots, alternating cords to create a net-like pattern that will serve as the main design of the runner.

4. If desired, add beads or decorative items by threading them onto the cords before tying knots to incorporate them into the design.

5. Periodically check the alignment and tension of the knots to ensure the runner lays flat and even.

Assembly and Finishing:

1. Once the desired length is achieved, finish the ends of the runner with a clean row of Square Knots to neatly gather and secure the final cords.

2. Trim any excess cord and, if desired, fray the ends to create a tassel effect along the edges of the runner.

3. Attach any additional embellishments strategically within the design to enhance the aesthetic appeal without overpowering the knotting.

Helpful Hints:

- Use a flat surface to layout the runner as you work, ensuring consistent tension and spacing.
- Choose a color scheme that complements your dining room decor or event theme.
- Consider the runner's placement and use when selecting materials, opting for more durable, stain-resistant cords if used frequently.

Expected Result: The finished Macramé table runner should be a beautiful piece showcasing simple yet elegant knotting techniques. It should lie flat on the table, providing a sophisticated and artistic centerpiece that enhances the overall dining experience. The patterns and optional embellishments should reflect the care and creativity put into the piece, making it not only a functional item but also a lovely addition to any home.

Decorative Pillows and Cushions

Project Goal: The aim of this project is to create decorative Macramé pillows and cushions that add a touch of handcrafted elegance to home decor. This project is perfect for beginners who want to craft stylish and comfortable accessories for lounges, bedrooms, or outdoor spaces.

Materials Needed:

- Cotton or hemp cord, 4mm thickness, about 150 feet for one medium-sized pillow

- Pillow form or stuffing material
- Scissors
- Measuring tape
- Optional: fabric backing for added durability and comfort

Knot Techniques Used:

- Lark's Head Knot
- Square Knot

Procedure:

Preparation of Materials:

1. Cut the cord into lengths of about 30 feet each. You will need approximately five lengths for a pillow cover that measures approximately 16x16 inches.
2. If using fabric backing, cut it to size to fit your pillow form, leaving extra for seam allowances.

Beginning the Work:

1. Start by creating a base grid of cords attached to a temporary frame or dowel using Lark's Head Knots. This grid will form the foundation of your pillow cover.

Project Development:

1. Begin the Macramé design by tying Square Knots along the grid, starting from one corner and working your way across to create the first row.
2. Continue with rows of Square Knots, ensuring even spacing and tension throughout to maintain a uniform design.
3. If desired, add simple patterns by alternating the starting points of the Square Knots in each row.

Assembly and Finishing:

1. Once the Macramé front of the pillow is complete, carefully remove it from the frame.
2. If using a fabric backing, sew the Macramé front to the fabric, right sides together, leaving an opening for the pillow form.
3. Turn the cover right side out, insert the pillow form, and hand-stitch the opening closed.

4. Trim any excess cords at the edges, and optionally, apply a fray-preventing solution to the ends.

Helpful Hints:

- Choose cords that are soft yet durable, especially if the pillows will be used frequently.
- Plan your design and measure your work area to ensure the final product will fit your pillow form accurately.
- If the pillows are intended for outdoor use, consider using materials that are weather-resistant and colorfast to avoid fading and wear.

Expected Result: The finished Macramé pillows should be attractive and comfortable, showcasing simple yet elegant patterns. They should fit snugly over the pillow form and maintain their shape and design integrity over time. These decorative pillows and cushions not only serve as functional pieces of home decor but also add a touch of handmade charm to any space.

Elegant Window Curtains

Project Goal: The goal of this project is to create beautiful Macramé window curtains that add a touch of handcrafted elegance to any room. This project is perfect for beginners who want to create decorative and functional window treatments.

Materials Needed:

- Cotton or hemp cord, 3mm thickness, about 400 feet for a standard window size
- Wooden dowel or curtain rod to hang the curtains
- Scissors
- Measuring tape
- Optional: wooden beads or rings for embellishment

Knot Techniques Used:

- Lark's Head Knot
- Square Knot
- Alternating Square Knot

Procedure:

Preparation of Materials:

1. Cut the cord into lengths of about 50 feet each. The number of cords will depend on the width of your window and the density of the curtain design.
2. If using embellishments, such as wooden beads or rings, ensure they are ready and suitable for threading onto the cords.

Beginning the Work:

1. Attach each cord to the wooden dowel or curtain rod using Lark's Head Knots. This setup will form the top of the curtain, where it hangs from the rod.

Project Development:

1. Begin the main body of the curtain by tying a foundation row of Square Knots below the dowel, using groups of four cords for each knot.
2. Incorporate rows of Alternating Square Knots to create a mesh-like structure. This design not only adds visual interest but also allows light to filter through.
3. Continue layering these knotting techniques, ensuring to keep the design symmetrical and balanced. The curtain should gradually expand in width slightly if a draped effect is desired.
4. If embellishments are part of your design, thread beads or rings onto specific cords at intervals, securing them with knots to ensure they stay in place.

Assembly and Finishing:

1. Once the curtain reaches the desired length, complete the design with a final row of Square Knots or a simple fringe at the bottom, depending on the style you prefer.
2. Trim any excess cord at the bottom and ensure all knots are tight and secure.
3. Hang the curtain on the rod and adjust it to ensure it drapes evenly and beautifully.

Helpful Hints:

- Consistently check the width and length against your window to ensure the curtain will fit perfectly.
- Use high-quality, durable cord that will withstand sunlight exposure if the window receives direct sunlight.
- Consider the overall decor style of the room when choosing cord color and embellishments to create a cohesive look.

Expected Result: The finished Macramé window curtain should be an elegant addition to your room decor, featuring simple knotting patterns that create visual interest and functional value. The patterns should be symmetrical, and the embellishments should add a touch of charm without overwhelming the design. This curtain will serve as both a window covering and a decorative piece that reflects the beauty of Macramé.

Bohemian Chic Bed Headboards

Project Goal: The goal of this project is to create a bohemian chic bed headboard that acts as a stylish focal point for any bedroom. This project is perfect for beginners who want to add a touch of handcrafted elegance with simple Macramé designs.

Materials Needed:

- Cotton or hemp cord, 5mm thickness, about 500 feet for a full-sized headboard
- A large wooden dowel or curtain rod, wider than the bed width, to serve as the headboard's top anchor
- Scissors
- Measuring tape
- Optional: wooden beads or other decorative elements for additional embellishment

Knot Techniques Used:

- Lark's Head Knot
- Square Knot
- Alternating Square Knot

Procedure:

Preparation of Materials:

1. Cut the cord into lengths of about 50 feet each, ensuring you have enough cords to cover the desired width and density of the headboard.
2. If using decorative elements like wooden beads, ensure they are suitable for threading onto the cords.

Beginning the Work:

1. Securely attach each cord to the wooden dowel using Lark's Head Knots, evenly spaced to ensure a uniform starting base.

Project Development:

1. Start by creating a foundation with several rows of Square Knots, forming a solid and sturdy base for the headboard.

2. Incorporate Alternating Square Knots to add variety and interest to the design. This pattern helps create a net-like structure that enhances the bohemian aesthetic.

3. Continue building the pattern, maintaining symmetry and balance in the design to complement the bedroom's style.

4. If using beads or other embellishments, thread them onto the cords at intervals and secure them with knots.

Assembly and Finishing:

1. Once the Macramé piece reaches the desired length, complete the end with a final row of Square Knots or let the cords hang freely for a relaxed, bohemian look.

2. Trim any excess cords at the bottom uniformly or in a pattern that complements the overall design of the headboard.

3. Secure the wooden dowel to the wall behind the bed, ensuring it is mounted at an appropriate height and is stable enough to support the weight of the Macramé.

Helpful Hints:

- Regularly step back and assess the work from a distance to ensure the design proportions are pleasing and fit well with the room's aesthetics.

- Choose a cord color that harmonizes with the bedroom palette to integrate the headboard seamlessly into the room.

- Be mindful of the weight of the headboard; ensure the mounting system is robust enough to safely hold the headboard in place.

Expected Result: The finished Macramé headboard should be an elegant and eye-catching feature of the bedroom, embodying a bohemian chic style with its simple yet stylish knotting patterns. The design should be balanced and harmonious, providing a beautiful focal point that enhances the room's ambiance. This headboard will serve as a stylish backdrop for the bed and showcase your Macramé skills.

Luxurious Bath Mats

Project Goal: The objective of this project is to create luxurious Macramé bath mats that combine functionality with a spa-like aesthetic. This project is perfect for beginners who want to craft a practical and decorative bathroom accessory.

Materials Needed:

- Cotton or other highly absorbent cord, 6mm thickness, about 200 feet for a medium-sized mat
- Scissors
- Measuring tape
- Non-slip mat backing (optional for added safety)

Knot Techniques Used:

- Lark's Head Knot
- Square Knot

Procedure:

Preparation of Materials:

1. Cut the cord into lengths of about 25 feet each. You will need approximately eight lengths for a medium-sized bath mat.
2. If using non-slip backing, prepare it by cutting it to match the size of the finished bath mat.

Beginning the Work:

1. Create a series of Lark's Head Knots across a temporary horizontal rod or dowel. This will form the top edge of the bath mat.

Project Development:

1. Start by weaving a foundation row of tight Square Knots just below the row of Lark's Head Knots. Use groups of four cords for each knot, ensuring they are closely spaced to create a dense and durable texture.
2. Continue adding rows of Square Knots to build the body of the mat. Maintain even tension and spacing to ensure a consistent and sturdy structure.
3. Periodically check the mat's dimensions and adjust your knotting technique as necessary to maintain the desired shape and size.

Assembly and Finishing:

1. Once the mat reaches the desired size, finish the final edge with a clean horizontal row of Square Knots, ensuring all cords are securely fastened.

2. Trim any excess cords and use a fray check solution or carefully melt the ends (if synthetic) to prevent fraying.

3. If using non-slip mat backing, attach it to the underside of the finished Macramé mat. This can be done by sewing or using a strong adhesive to ensure it stays in place and adds safety.

Helpful Hints:

- Choose a highly absorbent material for the cords, such as uncoated cotton, to ensure the mat is practical for bathroom use.

- Keep the mat flat during the knotting process to avoid curling or buckling.

- Consider the bathroom's color scheme and design when selecting the cord color to ensure the mat complements the existing decor.

Expected Result: The finished Macramé bath mat should be thick, absorbent, and luxurious, featuring simple yet effective knotting patterns that are both aesthetically pleasing and functional. The mat should lie flat against the floor with a non-slip backing to ensure safety and durability in a damp environment. This handcrafted bath mat not only serves as a practical bathroom accessory but also as a decorative piece that brings a touch of personalized luxury to the space.

Simple Jewelry Pieces

Project Goal: The objective of this project is to create simple Macramé jewelry pieces that introduce basic knotting techniques. This project is perfect for beginners who want to craft elegant, handmade jewelry such as bracelets, necklaces, or earrings.

Materials Needed:

- Fine Macramé thread or cord, 1mm thickness, various colors
- Jewelry findings (clasps, jump rings, earring hooks)
- Beads or small embellishments
- Scissors
- Measuring tape
- Jewelry pliers

Knot Techniques Used:

- Square Knot
- Lark's Head Knot

Procedure:

Preparation of Materials:

1. Select Macramé thread or cord in desired colors and cut into lengths appropriate for the type of jewelry being made (e.g., 4 feet for a bracelet, 6 feet for a necklace).
2. Prepare beads or small embellishments by organizing them according to size and color.

Beginning the Work:

1. Begin each piece by attaching the cord to a jewelry finding, such as a clasp or earring hook, using a secure Lark's Head Knot.

Project Development:

1. Start the design by tying a row of Square Knots to form the base structure of the jewelry piece, which could be a bracelet band, necklace chain, or earring body.
2. Thread beads onto the cord at intervals dictated by the design. Secure them in place by tying a Square Knot after each bead to prevent movement.
3. Continue adding Square Knots and beads, maintaining even spacing and tension to ensure the jewelry's shape and durability.

Assembly and Finishing:

1. As you approach the end of the piece, tie a final row of Square Knots to match the initial knots, ensuring symmetry.
2. Attach the end of the jewelry to the corresponding jewelry finding (e.g., the other half of the clasp) using a secure knot.
3. Trim any excess cord and carefully seal the ends with a dab of clear nail polish or jewelry glue to prevent fraying.
4. Optional: Add a focal bead or charm to the center of the piece if it fits the design.

Helpful Hints:

- Use high-quality, durable materials that are suitable for fine knotting to ensure the jewelry lasts and maintains its appearance over time.
- Regularly measure the piece against a ruler or wear it to check the fit and length, adjusting as necessary.

- Keep tools like pliers handy to help with attaching findings and handling small embellishments.

Expected Result: The finished Macramé jewelry pieces should be simple yet elegant, showcasing basic knotting work. Each piece should be structurally sound and aesthetically pleasing, with embellishments and findings securely attached. These handmade jewelry items enhance any outfit and reflect the creativity involved in their creation.

Simple Macramé Room Divider

Project Goal: The goal of this project is to create a simple Macramé room divider that adds a stylish touch to living spaces while subtly separating areas. This beginner-friendly project introduces basic knotting techniques to produce a functional and decorative piece for your home.

Materials Needed:
- Cotton or hemp cord, 6mm thickness, about 500 feet
- Wooden dowel or metal rod, length appropriate for the desired width of the divider
- Scissors
- Measuring tape
- Ceiling hooks or wall mounts for installation

Knot Techniques Used:
- Lark's Head Knot
- Square Knot

Procedure:

Preparation of Materials:

1. Cut the cord into lengths of about 50 feet each. You will need multiple strands depending on the width of the desired divider.
2. Prepare the wooden dowel or metal rod by ensuring it is smooth and free of splinters or sharp edges.

Beginning the Work:

1. Attach each cord to the dowel or rod using Lark's Head Knots, spacing them evenly to cover the entire length of the dowel.

Project Development:

1. Begin with a foundational row of Square Knots below the dowel, creating a solid base for the divider.
2. Continue adding more rows of Square Knots, maintaining even spacing and tension to build up the body of the divider.
3. Optionally, introduce simple patterns by alternating the direction of the Square Knots to add visual interest.

Assembly and Finishing:

1. Once the divider reaches the desired length, finish with a final row of Square Knots or a simple fringe at the bottom, depending on the style you prefer.
2. Trim any excess cord at the bottom and ensure all knots are tight and secure.
3. Install ceiling hooks or wall mounts at the appropriate locations, and hang the divider from the dowel or rod, making sure it is stable and evenly distributed.

Helpful Hints:

- Consider the weight of the finished divider and ensure the mounting system is robust enough to safely support it.
- Choose cord colors that complement or contrast with the room's color scheme to integrate the divider seamlessly into the space.
- Be mindful of the scale and placement of the divider, ensuring it effectively separates spaces without obstructing light or flow within the room.

Expected Result: The finished Macramé room divider should be a simple yet stylish piece that adds a touch of handcrafted charm to any room. It should be sturdy enough to stand as a semi-permanent fixture while adding a soft, textural element to the space. This divider not only serves the practical purpose of delineating areas but also acts as a decorative feature, showcasing the beauty of Macramé.

Detailed Chair Backings

Project Goal: The goal of this project is to create simple Macramé chair backings that add a touch of elegance to standard chairs. This beginner-friendly project introduces basic knotting techniques to enhance the aesthetic and comfort of your chairs.

Materials Needed:
- Cotton or hemp cord, 4mm thickness, about 100 feet for one chair backing
- Scissors
- Measuring tape
- Optional: wooden or metal beads for embellishment

Knot Techniques Used:
- Lark's Head Knot
- Square Knot

Procedure:

Preparation of Materials:

1. Cut the cord into lengths of about 25 feet each. You will need four lengths to cover the typical chair backing size.
2. If using, prepare beads or other embellishments by ensuring they can be threaded onto the cord and are suitable for the design.

Beginning the Work:
1. Measure the chair back to determine the exact size needed for the Macramé backing.
2. Attach each length of cord to a temporary horizontal dowel or rod using Lark's Head Knots. This setup will help maintain even tension and alignment during the knotting process.

Project Development:
1. Begin by creating a base with several rows of Square Knots. This base will provide structural stability and aesthetic consistency.
2. Continue adding rows of Square Knots to build up the body of the chair backing. Ensure that the knots are evenly spaced and tight to maintain a uniform appearance.
3. Optionally, integrate beads or embellishments into the knots to enhance the visual interest and uniqueness of the chair backing.

Assembly and Finishing:
1. Once the Macramé panel is complete, carefully remove it from the dowel.
2. Attach the finished Macramé backing to the chair by tying it directly to the chair frame or by affixing it with small hooks or ties, depending on the chair design.
3. Trim any excess cords and ensure all knots are secure.

4. Optional: Apply a fabric protector spray to enhance durability and resistance to wear, especially if the chair will be used frequently.

Helpful Hints:

- Maintain consistent knot tension throughout the project to ensure the backing is uniform and lays flat against the chair.
- Choose a cord color and bead embellishments that complement the chair and room decor.
- Regularly compare the work in progress to the chair to ensure a perfect fit and appropriate scale of the design.

Expected Result: The finished Macramé chair backing should be simple yet elegant, transforming an ordinary chair into a stylish piece of decor. The knots and optional embellishments should reflect basic craftsmanship, making the chair more beautiful and unique. This simple Macramé backing not only adds style and comfort to the chair but also showcases the versatility of Macramé.

Seasonal Projects

Christmas Tree Ornaments

Project Goal:

The objective of this project is to create unique and decorative Christmas tree ornaments using Macramé techniques. This seasonal project is perfect for crafters looking to add a personal touch to their holiday decor with intricate, handcrafted ornaments.

Materials Needed:

- Cotton or hemp cord, 2mm thickness, various colors (traditional holiday colors like red, green, white, or gold)
- Scissors
- Measuring tape
- Wooden beads, small bells, or other festive embellishments
- Metal or wooden rings (optional for hanging)

Knot Techniques Used:

- Lark's Head Knot
- Square Knot
- Spiral Knot
- Crown Knot (for creating spherical shapes)

Procedure:

Preparation of Materials:

1. Cut the cord into lengths of about 10 feet each. Adjust the length based on the size and complexity of the ornaments you plan to make.
2. Prepare any beads, bells, or other decorative items by ensuring they can be easily threaded onto the cord.

Beginning the Work:

1. If using a ring for hanging, begin by attaching cords to the ring using Lark's Head Knots. If not using a ring, fold each length of cord in half to form a loop for the top of the ornament.

Project Development:

1. Start with Square Knots to form a flat or slightly curved base for the ornament.
2. Introduce Spiral Knots to add a twisting, decorative texture as you work around or down the ornament.

3. For more intricate ornaments, use Crown Knots to create rounded or spherical designs that can be embellished or left simple.

4. Incorporate festive elements like wooden beads or small bells into your knots at intervals to enhance the holiday theme.

5. Continue with the chosen knotting techniques, shaping the ornament as desired, until it reaches the planned size and design.

Assembly and Finishing:

1. Finish off each ornament by securing all knots tightly and trimming excess cords to a neat finish.

2. If additional embellishments are to be added, attach them securely at this stage.

3. Optionally, apply a small loop of cord at the top for hanging if not using a pre-attached ring.

4. Optional: spray with a fabric stiffener to help the ornaments hold their shape better when hung on the tree.

Helpful Hints:

- Maintain even tension in your knots to ensure the ornaments are symmetrical and well-formed.

- Consider the overall design and color scheme of your Christmas tree when selecting cord colors and embellishments.

- Make a variety of designs to create a cohesive yet diverse collection of ornaments for display.

Expected Result: The finished Macramé Christmas tree ornaments should be charming and festive, showcasing detailed knotting and holiday-themed embellishments. Each ornament should be durable enough to be used year after year, adding a touch of handmade elegance to your holiday decor. These ornaments not only personalize your Christmas tree but also serve as lovely handmade gifts for friends and family.

Festive Garland Decorations

Project Goal:

The objective of this project is to create festive Macramé garland decorations that can adorn mantels, doorways, or walls during holiday celebrations. This seasonal project is ideal for crafters looking to add a handcrafted, festive touch to their decor with garlands featuring intricate knotting and holiday motifs.

Materials Needed:

- Cotton or hemp cord, 3mm thickness, in festive colors such as red, green, white, or metallics
- Scissors
- Measuring tape
- Wooden beads, stars, or other holiday-themed embellishments
- Small hooks or clips for hanging

Knot Techniques Used:

- Lark's Head Knot
- Square Knot
- Diagonal Half Hitch
- Picot Knot (for adding decorative loops)

Procedure:

Preparation of Materials:

1. Cut the cord into lengths of about 20 feet each, depending on the desired length of the garland.
2. Prepare embellishments by ensuring they are ready to be integrated into the garland—check that beads have large enough holes to thread onto the cord and that any other decorations are suitable for attaching.

Beginning the Work:

1. Begin by attaching the first length of cord to a fixed anchor point, such as a hook or nail, using a Lark's Head Knot to start with a secure base.

Project Development:

1. Start weaving the garland by tying a series of Square Knots to create a strong, flexible base for further embellishments.
2. Integrate Diagonal Half Hitches to create patterns or add texture to the garland. This knot is excellent for forming directional designs that add visual interest.
3. Use Picot Knots at intervals along the garland to create small, decorative loops that can hold additional decorations or add a lacy effect to the garland's design.
4. Thread wooden beads or hang small holiday-themed ornaments from the Picot loops or between sections of knots to enhance the festive look.
5. Continue with these knotting techniques, adding length and decorations until the garland reaches the desired length.

Assembly and Finishing:

1. Once the garland is complete, ensure all knots are tight and trim any excess cord for a neat finish.
2. Add hooks or clips at both ends of the garland for easy hanging.
3. Arrange the garland along a mantel, doorway, or wall, adjusting the drape and spacing of embellishments for the best visual effect.

Helpful Hints:

- Keep the spacing between knots consistent to maintain an even and balanced look.
- Choose cord and embellishments that are durable and can withstand handling, as garlands are often stored and reused.
- Be creative with color combinations and types of embellishments to make your garland unique and tailored to your holiday decor style.

Expected Result: The finished Macramé garland should be festive and eye-catching, with a harmonious blend of knots, beads, and holiday motifs. It should be sturdy enough to hang gracefully without sagging and versatile enough to be used in various decorative settings. This garland not only serves as a beautiful addition to your holiday decorations but also reflects the warmth and personal touch of handmade crafts.

Easter Basket Enhancements

Project Goal:

The aim of this project is to create beautiful Macramé enhancements for Easter baskets, adding a unique, handcrafted touch to traditional holiday decor. This seasonal project is perfect for those looking to personalize Easter baskets with intricate knotting that can hold Easter eggs, candies, or small gifts.

Materials Needed:

- Cotton or hemp cord, 2mm thickness, in pastel colors (e.g., pink, blue, yellow, lavender)
- Scissors
- Measuring tape
- Small wooden or ceramic eggs for decoration
- Optional: fabric dye to color the cords for added vibrancy

Knot Techniques Used:

- Lark's Head Knot
- Square Knot

- Spiral Knot
- Double Half Hitch

Procedure:

Preparation of Materials:

1. Cut the cord into lengths of about 10 feet each, depending on the size of the Easter baskets you intend to enhance.

2. If using, prepare the cords by dying them in pastel colors. Ensure the dye is set and dried completely before starting the Macramé work.

Beginning the Work:

1. Begin by wrapping a length of cord around the upper rim of the Easter basket, securing it in place with a series of Lark's Head Knots to create a stable base for further decoration.

Project Development:

1. After securing the base, continue with Square Knots to form a decorative band around the rim of the basket. This band serves as both a decorative element and additional support for the enhancements.

2. Integrate Spiral Knots below the initial band to add texture and a dynamic twist to the basket's appearance.

3. Use Double Half Hitches to create vertical or diagonal patterns along the sides of the basket, enhancing its depth and intricacy.

4. Optionally, thread small wooden or ceramic eggs onto the cords at intervals, securing them with knots. These embellishments add a thematic touch appropriate for Easter.

Assembly and Finishing:

1. Continue adding Macramé enhancements until the basket is adorned as desired. Make sure all knots and decorations are secure and evenly distributed around the basket.

2. Finish off the enhancement by tying off the ends of the cords neatly and discreetly underneath or along the inner rim of the basket.

3. Optional: Apply a light fabric stiffener to the cords if necessary to maintain the shape and ensure the enhancements hold up when the basket is filled.

Helpful Hints:

- Keep the enhancements proportional to the size of the Easter basket to ensure they complement rather than overwhelm it.

- Choose lightweight materials for any added decorations to prevent them from detaching or causing the basket to become top-heavy.

- Consider the end use of the basket, whether for display or for an Easter egg hunt, to ensure the enhancements are practical and durable.

Expected Result: The finished Easter basket should feature beautifully crafted Macramé enhancements that elevate its traditional appearance. The use of pastel-colored cords and thematic decorations like wooden eggs should integrate seamlessly with the spirit of Easter. These enhanced baskets are not only functional but also serve as charming holiday decor, perfect for showcasing Easter treats or as a centerpiece for holiday gatherings.

Halloween Themed Wall Art

Project Goal: The goal of this project is to create simple Halloween-themed Macramé wall art that adds a spooky yet stylish touch to holiday decorations. This beginner-friendly project features easy-to-make motifs like ghosts, pumpkins, and spider webs.

Materials Needed:

- Cotton or hemp cord, 4mm thickness, preferably in black, orange, and white
- Scissors
- Measuring tape
- Wooden dowel or branch to hang the art
- Optional: glow-in-the-dark beads or paint for a spooky effect

Knot Techniques Used:

- Lark's Head Knot
- Square Knot

Procedure:

Preparation of Materials:

1. Cut the cord into lengths of about 25 feet each, depending on the intended size of the wall art.
2. Prepare the wooden dowel or branch by cleaning and smoothing it to serve as the hanging base.

Beginning the Work:

1. Attach the cords to the dowel using Lark's Head Knots, spaced according to the design plan. Leave wider gaps for larger design elements like pumpkins or ghosts.

Project Development:

1. Outline the shape of your Halloween motifs (e.g., pumpkin, ghost, bat) using Square Knots to form the basic contours.

2. Fill in the shapes with more Square Knots to add texture and detail, like the lines on a pumpkin or the features of a ghost.

3. For spider web sections, create a simple net-like pattern by tying Square Knots at strategic points.

4. Optionally, integrate glow-in-the-dark beads or lightly brush areas with glow-in-the-dark paint to enhance the spooky effect under low light conditions.

5. Continue developing the piece, ensuring each part is securely knotted and supports the overall design.

Assembly and Finishing:

1. Once all elements are complete, ensure all knots are tight and the art piece maintains its intended shape.

2. Trim any excess cords at the bottom or sides of the piece to tidy up the appearance.

3. Secure the wooden dowel or branch for hanging, adding hooks or string as needed for easy installation.

4. Hang the finished wall art in a prominent place to complement other Halloween decorations.

Helpful Hints:

- Plan your design carefully to ensure that all elements are proportionate and harmoniously arranged within the available space.

- Use contrasting colors effectively to make each element pop, such as black for spider webs on a white background.

- Ensure that any glow-in-the-dark elements are exposed to light prior to display to maximize their glowing effect.

Expected Result: The finished Halloween-themed Macramé wall art should be a striking addition to your holiday decor, featuring simple, hand-knotted designs that capture the spirit of Halloween. The glow-in-the-dark accents should add a fun and eerie touch, making the piece a focal point of your decorations. This wall art not only celebrates the holiday but also showcases the creative potential of Macramé.

Valentine's Day Heart Wreaths

Project Goal:

The aim of this project is to create Valentine's Day heart-shaped wreaths using Macramé techniques. This seasonal project is ideal for crafters looking to decorate their space or gift a handmade piece that symbolizes love and affection with elegant, heart-shaped designs.

Materials Needed:

- Cotton or hemp cord, 3mm thickness, preferably in red, pink, or white
- Metal or wooden heart-shaped frame
- Scissors
- Measuring tape
- Optional: beads, ribbons, or artificial flowers for embellishment

Knot Techniques Used:

- Lark's Head Knot
- Square Knot
- Alternating Square Knot
- Spiral Knot
- Gathering Knot

Procedure:

Preparation of Materials:

1. Cut the cord into lengths of about 20 feet each, depending on the size of the heart-shaped frame and the density of the knots desired.
2. Prepare any embellishments such as beads, ribbons, or flowers that you may want to incorporate into the design.

Beginning the Work:

1. Attach cords to the heart-shaped frame using Lark's Head Knots, spacing them evenly around the entire perimeter of the frame.

Project Development:

1. Start with a series of Square Knots following the shape of the frame to create a solid base layer that defines the heart shape clearly.
2. Add texture and depth by incorporating Alternating Square Knots and Spiral Knots. Use these techniques to fill in the heart shape, ensuring that the knots are tight and the shape is maintained.

3. For sections where more intricate patterns or designs are desired, use Diagonal Half Hitches to create finer details or to add a lacy effect.

4. Integrate any beads or small embellishments into the knots at this stage to enhance the festive, romantic feel of the wreath.

5. As you work, adjust and tighten the knots to ensure that the wreath maintains its shape and the cords do not sag.

Assembly and Finishing:

1. Once the Macramé work covers the entire frame and you are satisfied with the design, finish off by securing all ends with Gathering Knots where necessary.

2. Trim any excess cord and tuck in the ends to keep the back of the wreath neat.

3. Decorate the wreath with optional ribbons or artificial flowers, attaching them securely to the frame or weaving them through the Macramé knots.

4. Add a loop of cord at the top of the wreath for hanging.

Helpful Hints:

- Ensure the heart frame is robust enough to support the weight of the Macramé knots and embellishments.

- Use contrasting colors or varied shades of red and pink to add visual interest and depth to the wreath.

- Consider the wreath's placement (e.g., indoors or outdoors) when selecting materials to ensure durability and weather resistance if needed.

Expected Result: The finished Valentine's Day heart wreath should be visually striking and embody the spirit of the holiday, with a beautifully knotted heart shape that can be displayed on doors, walls, or windows. The additional embellishments should complement the Macramé work without overwhelming it, creating a balanced and appealing decoration. This wreath not only serves as a charming Valentine's Day decor but also as a heartfelt handmade gift that can be cherished year after year.

Simple Thanksgiving Table Centerpieces

Project Goal: The aim of this project is to create simple Thanksgiving table centerpieces using basic Macramé techniques. This beginner-friendly project adds a warm, handcrafted touch to your Thanksgiving decor, incorporating autumnal elements for a festive table setting.

Materials Needed:

- Cotton or hemp cord, 4mm thickness, in autumn colors like burnt orange, deep red, brown, and golden yellow
- Scissors
- Measuring tape
- A base structure, such as a ring or a series of interconnected rings or frames
- Optional: pine cones, artificial leaves, small pumpkins, and other Thanksgiving-themed decorations

Knot Techniques Used:

- Lark's Head Knot
- Square Knot

Procedure:

Preparation of Materials:

1. Cut the cord into lengths of about 15 feet each. You will need several lengths depending on the size of the centerpiece.
2. Prepare additional decorative elements like pine cones and artificial leaves by ensuring they can be easily attached to the Macramé structure.

Beginning the Work:

1. Attach cords to the base structure (ring or frame) using Lark's Head Knots, spacing them evenly to cover the entire base.

Project Development:

1. Start with a series of Square Knots around the base structure to create a solid foundation.
2. Continue adding more rows of Square Knots to build up the body of the centerpiece, keeping the knots tight and evenly spaced.
3. If desired, incorporate Thanksgiving-themed decorations like small pumpkins or pine cones by tying them into the knots or hanging them from the structure.
4. Add more layers of Square Knots until the centerpiece reaches the desired size and fullness.

Assembly and Finishing:

1. Once the Macramé covering is complete and all decorative elements are in place, finish the edges by tying off the cords with simple knots.

2. Trim any excess cord and tuck in loose ends for a neat finish.

3. Place the centerpiece on the Thanksgiving table and arrange additional decor elements around it, such as candles or a burlap table runner, to enhance the festive atmosphere.

Helpful Hints:

- Keep the design simple and symmetrical for an elegant look.

- Use sturdy materials that can support the weight and structure of added decorations.

- Choose colors that match or complement your existing Thanksgiving decor to create a cohesive look.

Expected Result: The finished Thanksgiving table centerpiece should be a lovely addition to your holiday table, featuring warm colors and simple Macramé patterns. The integration of natural and thematic decorations should evoke the essence of Thanksgiving, making the dining experience more festive and inviting. This centerpiece not only serves as a decorative focus but also showcases the beauty of Macramé in a seasonal context.

New Year's Eve Party Favors

Project Goal:

The objective of this project is to create unique and festive New Year's Eve party favors using Macramé techniques. These small, handcrafted items will add a personalized touch to your celebration, serving as memorable keepsakes for guests.

Materials Needed:

- Cotton or hemp cord, 2mm thickness, in metallic colors like gold, silver, and black

- Scissors

- Measuring tape

- Small rings or clasps for attaching to keys or bags

- Optional: small beads, charms, or sequins to add sparkle and festivity

Knot Techniques Used:

- Lark's Head Knot

- Square Knot

- Spiral Knot

- Crown Knot

Procedure:

Preparation of Materials:

1. Cut the cord into lengths of about 6 feet each, which is ample for small keychain-sized favors.
2. If using, prepare beads, charms, or sequins by ensuring they can be threaded onto the cord or attached securely.

Beginning the Work:

1. Begin by attaching the cord to a small ring or clasp using a Lark's Head Knot, ensuring it's secure as this will be the top of the party favor.

Project Development:

1. Start with a sequence of Square Knots immediately below the ring to create a sturdy and decorative base.
2. Incorporate Spiral Knots to add a dynamic, twisted pattern, giving the favor a festive look and feel.
3. Introduce beads or charms intermittently between knots for sparkle and to emphasize the New Year's theme. This can include numbers for the coming year, stars, or other relevant symbols.
4. If creating a more spherical shape, use Crown Knots towards the bottom of the favor to round off the design, making it compact and suitable for carrying.

Assembly and Finishing:

1. Complete the design by securing the end with a final Square Knot or a Gathering Knot if ending with a tassel.
2. Trim any excess cord and ensure all embellishments are tightly fastened to prevent loss during use.
3. If desired, add a drop of glue to knot ends to prevent fraying, especially if the favors will be used as keychains.

Helpful Hints:

- Keep the favors small and lightweight for ease of distribution and use.
- Choose colors and materials that reflect the New Year's Eve theme, opting for brightness and sparkle where possible.
- Consider the overall design and practicality, ensuring each favor is both decorative and durable.

Expected Result: The finished New Year's Eve party favors should be stylish and functional, reflecting the celebratory and hopeful spirit of the occasion. Each favor should be crafted with attention to detail, offering your guests a unique keepsake that commemorates the celebration. These Macramé favors not only serve as a festive accessory but also demonstrate thoughtful craftsmanship, making the New Year's Eve party memorable for everyone involved.

Fourth of July Bunting

Project Goal: The aim of this project is to create simple and festive Fourth of July bunting using basic Macramé techniques. This project is perfect for beginners looking to add a handcrafted touch to their Independence Day celebrations with red, white, and blue colors.

Materials Needed:
- Cotton or hemp cord, 3mm thickness, in red, white, and blue
- Scissors
- Measuring tape
- Wooden dowels or small rods to support the bunting structure
- Optional: stars or other patriotic embellishments

Knot Techniques Used:
- Lark's Head Knot
- Square Knot

Procedure:

Preparation of Materials:
1. Cut the cord into lengths of about 10 feet each, enough for several flags or sections in the bunting.
2. If using embellishments like stars, ensure they can be easily attached to the Macramé design.

Beginning the Work:
1. Attach each length of cord to the wooden dowels or rods using Lark's Head Knots, spacing them evenly for the number of flags or sections planned.

Project Development:
1. Start by creating a foundation of Square Knots immediately below the dowel. This establishes a strong base for each flag or section.

2. Continue with more rows of Square Knots to form the main body of each flag, adding length and developing the triangular or rectangular shape typical of bunting.

3. Optionally, add patterns or stripes using alternating colors of red, white, and blue cords.

Assembly and Finishing:

1. Once each section is complete, ensure all knots are tight and the overall design is consistent.

2. Trim any excess cord at the ends of each flag or section and finish with a neat fray or tassel if desired.

3. Attach the dowels or rods securely to a length of cord or string at the top, spacing them evenly to ensure the bunting hangs correctly.

4. Hang the bunting in a prominent place, such as along a fence, across a porch, or above a gathering area, to enhance the festive atmosphere.

Helpful Hints:

- Keep the designs simple and focused on the theme to clearly convey the patriotic spirit of the Fourth of July.

- Use weather-resistant materials if the bunting will be displayed outdoors to ensure it withstands elements like sunlight and rain.

- Consider the installation method and location to determine the best way to secure the bunting safely and attractively.

Expected Result: The finished Fourth of July bunting should be vibrant and celebratory, showcasing simple Macramé work in patriotic colors. It should serve as a decorative focal point for Independence Day celebrations, enhancing the festive atmosphere with its handcrafted quality. This bunting not only adds to the holiday decor but also demonstrates the versatility of Macramé as a decorative art form suitable for seasonal celebrations.

Chapter 3: Design Your Own Patterns

Diving into the art of Macramé with the intention to design your own patterns is an exciting venture that blends traditional techniques with personal expression. This journey calls for a deep understanding of the foundational knots and an imaginative approach to reassembling them into something uniquely your own. As you prepare to infuse your creativity into every loop and twist, you embark on a path that not only challenges your skills but also enhances your connection to this age-old craft, transforming simple cords into extraordinary works of art.

Principles of Pattern Design

In the realm of Macramé, designing your own patterns is akin to charting unexplored territories—each choice and innovation shapes the landscape of your final creation. The art of pattern design in Macramé is not merely a process of aesthetic arrangement but an exploration of personal expression and creativity. By understanding and applying the fundamental principles of pattern design, you cultivate a landscape where intuition and technique flourish side by side, giving birth to uniquely personal and expressive works of art.

At the heart of effective pattern design lies the principle of balance. Balance is the silent symphony conductor, ensuring that each element, whether a knot or a space, contributes to a harmonious whole without overwhelming it. Think of your Macramé piece as a seesaw, with visual elements on either side; your goal is to distribute these elements so the seesaw sits level, creating visual peace that is pleasing to the eye. This can mean alternating knot types across the work, or it might involve symmetrical designs where each half mirrors the other.

Contrast is another pillar of pattern design, acting as the spice that adds depth to your creations. By varying knot sizes, cord thickness, and color, you can highlight specific areas of your work, guiding the observer's eye to focal points that define the piece's character. Contrast is not just about opposition but about complementation—darker, thicker cords can make a delicate, light pattern stand out, just as a bold, busy section can make a simpler, serene part pop.

Repetition is the rhythm of your design, the recurring beat that provides structure and familiarity within the piece. It builds patterns that are recognizable and comfortable, yet it needs to be used judiciously. Too much repetition can lead to monotony, while too little may result in visual chaos. Striking the right balance involves repeating elements just enough to create a motif without stifling creativity or dynamism within the overall design.

Proportion and scale are crucial when considering the impact of your work. They dictate the relationship between different elements of your design, ensuring that each part contributes to the overall aesthetic without dominating it. In Macramé, this might mean choosing smaller knots to create delicate, intricate accessories, or larger, more robust knots for a statement piece of wall art. Proportion also influences the perception of space within the piece, where larger scaled knots can make a piece feel more 'open' and smaller knots can make it feel 'tighter' and more detailed.

Unity and variety must also coexist within your designs. Unity ensures that all parts of your Macramé piece feel cohesive, a single entity rather than a random assembly of knots and cords. Variety, meanwhile, keeps the viewer's interest alive, injecting life and energy into the piece. Achieving this can mean introducing unexpected knots or colors in a rhythm that still aligns with the overall design, or it can involve thematic variations on a standard knot pattern.

Finally, the principle of emphasis, or focus, directs the viewer's attention to the heart of your design. This can be achieved by isolating a particular knot pattern, using a striking color, or placing an unusual texture at strategic points within the piece. Emphasis ensures that, regardless of the complexity of the design, there is a clear point that captures and holds the viewer's interest, making a statement that resonates with emotional or aesthetic power.

Designing your own patterns in Macramé requires a blend of adherence to these principles and the courage to experiment beyond them. Each piece you create is a dialogue between the fibers you knot and the space you shape, guided by these foundational concepts but driven by your unique creative vision.

As you wield these principles with confidence and creativity, you will find that designing patterns is not just about following rules but about interpreting them in ways that speak uniquely to and from your artistic soul. Each new design is a step further in your Macramé journey, a testament to your evolving skills and deepening connection with this expressive art form. Your patterns are more than just arrangements of knots; they are personal signatures, indelible marks of your creativity on the canvas of Macramé.

Creating Custom Projects

Venturing into the creation of custom Macramé projects is akin to setting off on a bespoke artistic journey, one where your personal narrative and aesthetic preferences guide every choice and knot. This pursuit is not merely about crafting something beautiful; it's an exploration of personal expression through the tactile and therapeutic art of knotting. It involves a deep engagement with the materials, a dialogue with design principles, and a commitment to bringing a unique vision to life.

The process of creating custom Macramé projects begins with inspiration, that spark that ignites the imagination and fuels the desire to create. Inspiration can come from myriad sources: the natural world with its organic patterns and textures, architectural forms with their strong lines and symmetry, or even historical tapestries that echo ancient crafts. Allow these sparks to form the foundation of your project, translating them into a language of cords and knots that resonates with personal meaning.

Once inspired, the next step involves meticulous planning. This phase is crucial as it involves transforming abstract ideas into tangible outcomes. Begin by sketching your designs, playing with arrangements of knots and considering the flow of the overall piece. This visual blueprint serves not only as a guide throughout the crafting process but also helps in troubleshooting potential issues early in the design phase.

Choosing the right materials is next and is as vital as the design itself. The cords you select—be they cotton, hemp, or jute—should not only complement the aesthetic you aim to achieve but also suit the functional purpose of the project. For example, choosing a more durable cord like nylon for items that will be used outdoors can extend the life of your project, while softer, more pliable cords can be ideal for wearable items like jewelry.

The scale of your project also influences your choice of materials and the complexity of your designs. Larger projects like wall hangings or curtains may allow for bolder, more dramatic knotting patterns, whereas smaller projects like bracelets and coasters call for finer, more delicate knots. Each project's scale will guide how intricate or simple your knotting techniques should be to achieve the desired impact.

As you begin knotting, consider the structural integrity of your piece. This involves not just the strength of the knots themselves but also their functionality in the context of the item's use. For instance, a Macramé plant hanger must be able to support weight, requiring secure knots and perhaps a double layer of cord, whereas a decorative piece might focus more on aesthetic knot patterns and color variations.

Throughout the creation process, maintain a flexible attitude. Often, the material or the design may not behave as anticipated. The texture of the cord might influence the knot's appearance, or the weight of the finished product might require adjustments in the design. These moments call for creativity and problem-solving, turning potential challenges into unique features of your custom project.

Attention to finishing touches is what can elevate a custom Macramé project from good to great. This includes not just the trimming of excess cords or the addition of accessories like beads or tassels but also considering how the piece will be displayed or used. Adding a hidden loop for hanging or incorporating adjustable knots for wearable items can greatly enhance the functionality and aesthetic of the final piece.

Finally, reflect on the completed project as a step in your ongoing creative evolution. Each custom piece is a repository of learned skills and experimented techniques, a physical manifestation of your artistic growth. Take time to assess what worked well and what could be improved, storing these insights for use in future projects.

Creating custom Macramé projects is more than just a crafting endeavor; it's a personal journey that blends artistry with introspection. It's about making something that stands out as a singular testament to your creative abilities and vision, a tangible connection between your hands and your heart. As you progress, each knot tied not only brings your design to life but also tightens your connection to the craft, weaving your story into the expansive tapestry of Macramé.

As the last knot is tied and your pattern comes to completion, you stand back to witness not just a series of interconnected cords, but a personal stamp on a traditional craft. This chapter in your Macramé journey underscores the beauty of individual expression within the bounds of knotting techniques. Each project you undertake from here enriches your understanding and stretches your creativity, allowing you to weave not just threads, but also stories and memories into patterns that resonate with your unique artistic voice. Through this process, you become not just a follower of patterns but a creator, continuously pushing the boundaries of what you can design and achieve with Macramé.

Acknowledgments

Every book, much like every tapestry of Macramé, is woven from the threads of inspiration, support, and collective endeavor that connect the solitary act of writing to the wider world of shared experience. In creating "Macramé for Beginners," the fabric of my journey has been richly adorned by many who have contributed their threads of wisdom, encouragement, and guidance.

At the forefront of this supportive community is my family, whose unwavering belief in my artistic endeavors has been nothing short of foundational. My partner, whose patience and understanding knew no bounds, provided the quiet, essential support that allowed me to pursue late-night bursts of creativity and overcome the inevitable challenges of a detailed craft. To my children, who have grown up amidst piles of cords and the gentle clatter of wooden beads, your youthful enthusiasm and awe for each completed piece have reminded me of the joy at the heart of creation. Your curiosity has often reignited my own, pushing me to explore further and with more courage.

My gratitude extends deeply to my mentor, whose teachings were instrumental in shaping not only the techniques that fill these pages but also my philosophy towards craft and community. Her rigorous standards and compassionate teaching style imbued in me a profound respect for the discipline of Macramé, inspiring me to pass on this knowledge with integrity and warmth. Her belief in sustainability as an integral part of crafting has particularly resonated with me, shaping much of the work I do today.

The vibrant community of fellow Macramé artists and enthusiasts has also been crucial in bringing this book to fruition. From the lively exchanges on online forums to the collaborative projects at craft fairs, your shared insights and feedback have been invaluable. To those who participated in the initial workshops where I tested the tutorials that now lie within these pages—your questions, challenges, and successes helped refine each step into a clearer, more accessible form.

Special thanks are due to my editor, whose keen eye and thoughtful suggestions have made this book far stronger and more coherent. Your ability to weave through the technicalities of Macramé while keeping an eye on the reader's learning experience has been incredible. Your dedication is evident on every page, and I am immensely grateful for your commitment.

I am also profoundly thankful to the local artisans who supplied the sustainable and ethically sourced materials that I used throughout the projects featured in this book. Your commitment to quality and the environment resonates deeply with my work, and your beautiful materials have not only inspired but have also elevated the aesthetic appeal of every project showcased here.

A heartfelt acknowledgment must go to the photography team, whose photography has brought the text to life. Your ability to capture the essence of Macramé in every shot provides not just a visual guide but also an inspiration to readers. The beauty of your work has made this book a piece of art in itself.

Lastly, I extend my thanks to you, the reader, for picking up this book and embarking on your own Macramé journey. May the knots you tie bring as much joy and fulfillment to your life as they have to mine. This book is not just a collection of projects and patterns; it is an invitation to weave your own stories, to create connections, and to build a community through the shared love of crafting.

Each of you mentioned, and countless others unnamed, have touched this project in ways both big and small. Like the intricate knots of Macramé, your influences are interlaced throughout the very essence of this book, making it a true collective masterpiece. Thank you all for being part of this incredibly rewarding journey.

SCAN THE QR CODE:

OR COPY AND PASTE THE URL:

https://bit.ly/46Wtfem

Made in the USA
Las Vegas, NV
07 December 2024

13565259R00059